SpringerBriefs in Criminology

For further volumes:
http://www.springer.com/series/10159

Shahid Alvi

Youth Criminal Justice Policy in Canada

A Critical Introduction

 Springer

Prof. Shahid Alvi
Faculty of Social Science and Humanities
University of Ontario Institute of Technology
55 Bond Street East
Oshawa, Ontario
L1G OA5
Canada
e-mail: shahid.alvi@uoit.ca

ISSN 2192-8533   e-ISSN 2192-8541
ISBN 978-1-4419-0272-6   e-ISBN 978-1-4419-0273-3
DOI 10.1007/978-1-4419-0273-3
Springer New York Dordrecht Heidelberg London

Library of Congress Control Number: 2011938641

Cover design: eStudio Calamar, Berlin/Figueres

Printed on acid-free paper

Springer is part of Springer Science+Business Media (www.springer.com)

Dedicated To PJC, E and M

Introduction

Although this short book is generally aimed at students of youth crime, I want to broaden the conversation to include youth who may not be guests of the criminal justice system, but who are nevertheless part of a drift towards punitiveness and social exclusion in Canada.

There are many reasons that Canadian social policy has drifted in this direction. This book describes that drift, its consequences, and where we might go from here. In Chap. 1, I examine the criminalization of youth in early Canada up to the present day. I provide a historical discussion of youth in Canada, paying attention to the widely accepted idea that concepts such as youth, teenagers, pre-teens, and children are social constructions reflecting broader social and cultural values and conditions. As with concepts like gender and "race," social constructionist theorists have long pointed to the ways in which such seemingly objective social phenomena are in fact manifestations of what Berger and Luckmann (1967) call "nomos building"—the process by which people try to impose "meaningful order on experience" which in turn is crucial to the larger project of making official versions of reality come to be taken for granted. Yet such processes are themselves subject to situations in which the "taken for granted" becomes problematic and new versions of reality are constructed in response. In this chapter, then, I attempt to paint a picture of the changing concept of youth and childhood, and how these shifting definitions in turn have been reflected in social and youth justice policy.

In Chap. 2, my objective is to provide an empirical account of young people's experiences of being young in the current economic and social context. In addition, these data are presented in the context of the broader drift in late capitalist societies towards hyper-individuation, the widening gap between the rich and the poor, and the contradictory tendency to deal with these issues by conjuring up policies that at best, offer us more of the same. The chapter then turns to the broader problem of the social exclusion of youth in Canada. Drawing upon the recent work of John Muncie (2008), and Elliott Currie (2004), I focus on what scholars have called the "punitive turn," both within families and within the broader social structure in which the criminal justice system is embedded.

Having presented what I hope will be a useful contextual framework for understanding contemporary youth deviance and criminality, Chap. 3 offers data on the nature and contours of youth offending. I do not wish to provide an overview of the myriad theories that have evolved over many decades purporting to explain youth crime. That task has been accomplished admirably in numerous textbooks and monographs. Instead, I want to draw upon and connect the issues discussed in Chaps. 1 and 2 with these data to offer a critical perspective on youth crime. I provide a set of criteria with which to weigh the validity and reliability of such theories, and then provide a provisional perspective on the causal nexus.

In the fourth and final chapter, I provide a policy agenda that addresses the issues explored earlier in the book. I have always argued that we cannot expect to solve crime with law. Yet increasingly, Canadians have witnessed an almost obsessive compulsion on the part of policy and law makers to trivialize the realities of young people's existence by making and attempting to enforce harsh, harmful, and ultimately ineffective laws. It is my hope that this book will provide a fresh perspective on what in my view has come to be an increasingly narrow conversation on the role of youth in our society, why they sometimes fail to "measure up," and what we can do about it.

Finally, this book was originally supposed to be an updated version of a book I had written on youth and the Canadian criminal justice system in 1999. Since that time, the main legislation governing youth crime has changed. But as I began to plan this book, I realized that although the legislation had changed so too had many other things. Although I borrow heavily from the material I wrote back in 1999, this volume adds other layers to my analysis of the social forces and conditions that shape Canada's youth and children and attempts to integrate this analysis with the broader theme of social control, as well as with the criminal justice response to young people's transgressions.

A Critical Approach to Youth Justice

There is no question that understanding and responding to crime requires taking what goes on in the minds or bodies of individuals seriously, but as with some sociological theories, the case for individual biological or psychological factors is too often overstated. Biological and psychological theories of crime do help us to understand some aspects of, and some types of crime, but fail to explain many other more common crimes, and most variants tend to ignore the relationship between social factors and biological and psychological functioning.

The policy implications of these perspectives focus on treatment and rehabilitation. And while many sociologists by and large support such programs, they also argue that our response to crime should attempt to change the social environment in which biological and psychological factors interact. Kelly (1996: 467) puts the matter more strongly, arguing that treatment programs focusing exclusively on the individual are usually unsuccessful because policy makers and practitioners have failed to recognize that those being "treated" exist in a social world, to which they must return after treatment. That social world has made demands on them. It has played a central role in making that person who they are, and it will continue to do so after the individual has been "rehabilitated." To ignore this is to completely misunderstand the realities of that individual's life. Not surprisingly, when individual treatment fails the fault is seen as residing with the individual, not in social terms, ironically perpetuating a hopeless cycle of failure. In addition, ignoring the individual's immediate social environment such as peers, parents, and school may be one thing, but individualized treatment cannot deal with the *larger* social environment in which peers, parents, schools, and the offender exist. Put another way, individualized "solutions" to youth crime ignore *larger* social, political, and economic factors, such as the way market societies operate to create schools that set students up for "success" and "failure," marginalize those who do not meet "standards," or create conditions under which families live in poverty from which there is little likelihood of escape.

Thus, this short volume examines youth crime in the context of a critical perspective on youth and society. What does it mean to take a "critical" perspective within criminology? Beginning with the idea that society is characterized by conflict between interest groups over values and resources, critical criminologists argue that it is impossible to separate one's principles from the criminological enterprise (Schwartz and Friedrichs 1994). It is argued that all perspectives on crime have inherent biases towards particular views of the world. Hence, critical criminologists *choose* to examine crime on behalf of the underprivileged or weak. Further, because they locate the causes of crime in the nature of the social structure, critical criminological perspectives generally seek solutions to crime in radically *transforming* the social structure. This book has a specifically Marxist/critical orientation which in itself is a multi-faceted approach.

Critical theories, including those that could be called Marxist in orientation, start with the idea that people make decisions and choices about their actions and lives, but within circumstances they have *not* chosen themselves. Put another way, young people may well choose to commit violent crimes, but critical theorists would be interested in the ways in which social structural factors (such as poverty, dropping out of school, or some other disadvantage) contributed to that youth's decision to commit his or her crime.

Beginning with the idea that human beings are conditioned by their social circumstances, critical theories maintain that factors like exploitation, alienation, power, and social class are central to an understanding of crime, and that crime is a "rational response" to the demands of capitalist society (Gordon 1973; Greenberg 1981). Moreover, such approaches maintain that people learn to commit crime in circumstances where their attachment to the conventional social world has broken down and when they lack legitimate opportunities to participate in conventional social life. Unlike more mainstream theories, however, marxist approaches locate factors like juvenile offenders, their peers, schools, families, and the strain they experience, *within the context of capitalist social relations*. It is capitalism as a social system, and the relationships that exist within and characterize this system that in the final analysis, are responsible for crime.

For instance, *left idealists* would contend that many youth who commit crime are simply reacting to their position in the class structure. They have little connection with the working world, little or no hope for the future, and diminished life chances and so their crime is a reaction to their circumstances. They are, in effect, modern day "Robin Hoods," whose actions symbolize the plight of the working and underprivileged classes and their resistance to the political and economic system (capitalism) that represses them (DeKeseredy and Schwartz 1996).

There are many criticisms of this position. One of the most important is the empirical fact that the vast majority of crimes committed by working class people victimize other working class individuals, and not the middle or capitalist classes which repress them. Another problem with left idealism is its tendency to assume that being poor or working class automatically predisposes one to commit crime. Again, however, we know empirically that not all poor young people commit crimes and we also know that many harmful crimes are committed by the wealthy and powerful in our society.

Because they dismiss working class crime as inconsequential and as "proto-revolutionary" activity, idealists focus too much attention on crimes of the powerful, thereby ignoring some crucial realities. Moreover, because street crime is ignored in this way, and since the causes of crime are said to be so fundamentally rooted in the nature of capitalism, idealists tend to have very few concrete proposals for reducing crime. Instead, they argue that nothing short of a fundamental "revolution" in the way we produce, a transformation to socialism, will solve the problem of crime once and for all.

More recent, neo-marxist theories of youth crime have made some advances over left idealism. Colvin and Pauly (1983) maintain that adults experiences of authority and control at the workplace create particular perceptions and responses to authority in general. These bonds are translated into family relationships between parents and parents and children, and are reinforced by educational and peer experiences. In short, delinquency is a consequence of the authority bonds that exist in workers' lives. While conditional empirical support for this theory has been found, it remains relatively untested and ignores a range of other factors that contribute to juvenile crime, particularly gender (Simpson and Elis 1994).

More recently, Colvin (1996) argues that crime is linked to the process of social reproduction, defined as involving the institutions of socialization that prepare people for productive roles in society (1996: 60). When such institutions fail to prepare youth for participation in the economy, society loses the productive potential of these individuals, experiences higher costs of welfare and prisons, and higher rates of crime and other social pathologies. Thus, Colvin takes the explicitly marxist position that crime is a consequence of social structural inequality stemming from the class structure of capitalist society which in turn determines the priorities and resources allocated to major institutions of socialization such as families and schools. Kids who do not do well in school or go to disadvantaged schools, hang out with peers in the same social situation and who come from disadvantaged families are more likely to commit crime.

The keys to reducing crime, then, include better supports for the poor, comprehensive job training, nationwide parent-effectiveness programs, preschool programs, expanded and enhanced public education, service programs that encourage youth to participate in adult and community life, enhanced workplace environments emphasizing democratic control, collective bargaining which encourage the development of self-directed, creative employees, economic investment in industries meeting human needs and services, and a more progressive income tax system (Colvin 1996).

Left realists take some of the arguments made by idealists seriously, but build a much more "practical" or "realistic" theory of crime and what is to be done about it. In addition to arguing that crime is a serious problem for the working class, John Lea and Jock Young (1984: 81) two of realism's most important defenders, argue that the cause of crime can be placed in the context of the equation, Relative Deprivation = Discontent, Discontent + Political Marginalization = Crime. Discontent is a product of relative deprivation because it occurs when comparisons between comparable groups are made which suggests that unnecessary injustices are occurring. Relative deprivation is the notion that people perceive their position in society in different ways and relative to other people. For instance, poor people might not view themselves as worse off than others *if everyone* around them is poor, but in the midst of a society that is blatantly unequal, their perspective might be different. It is "poverty experienced as unfair (relative deprivation when compared to someone else) that creates discontent" (1984: 88). For Lea and Young, political marginalization consists of two components: "isolation from the effective channels of pressure-group politics, and isolation from processes whereby political interests can be clearly and instrumentally formulated" (1984: 214).

In addition, left realists use the metaphor of the "square of crime," to illustrate the relationships between key people and institutions in the study of crime. The square consists of 1. the state, which is responsible for law-making, policing, and sentencing, 2. the general public, which reacts to crime, 3. the offender, and 4. the victim. Thus, Young (1992: 27) argues that:It is the relationship between the police and the public which determines the efficacy of policing, the relationship between the victim and the offender which determines the impact of crime, the relationship between the state and the offender which is a major factor in recidivism.

The implications of this theory are particularly interesting for understanding youth crime because most young people are socialized to believe that the future holds promise, that it can be realized with a little hard work, and that failure to achieve these goals is a failure of the individual, not the system. When their expectations are not fulfilled, they replace legitimate and conventional interests with a "diffuse set of resentments and grievances"—they become discontented. This discontent, when combined with the inability to change things through legitimate avenues (such as voting, or through access to powerful interest groups), and in conjunction with relative deprivation, greatly increases the chances of criminal activity among youth.

In summary, then, left realists argue that crime is not just a "moral panic" manufactured by the ruling elite. To be sure, they argue, we should take crimes of the powerful seriously, but we should also focus on the fact that working class people are victimized by the powerful and other members of the working class in capitalist society. Moreover, crime is a relational phenomenon that demonstrates the anti-social nature of our society.

Left realism has been subject to a number of criticisms, including the fact that it may have departed too far in philosophical orientation from its more left-wing counterpart in left idealism. As a consequence, some may claim that left realism is nothing more than liberal theory in a new guise—there is nothing "left" about left realism. A related concern is that in claiming to offer a realistic strategy for reducing crime and the harm it causes, realists must automatically engage with, and potentially embrace current strategies that are conservative and oppressive (Schwartz 1991). In addition, some, such as Einstadter and Henry (1995) have argued that realists focus too much on working class crime and not enough on crimes of the powerful. Others have claimed that the left realist perspective on the role of the community in responding to crime assumes that our communities are homogeneous rather than diverse, and that the potential for individuals with particular interests might create a strategy as oppressive as the current system (Michalowski 1991).

Since realists focus on access to legitimate opportunities for self-fulfillment, as well as political expression, the practical implications, particularly for youth justice are similar to other theories emphasizing inequality.

The solution to crime, according to Lea and Young, consists of:

- The *demarginalization* of offenders by providing alternatives to prison and which serve to *integrate* the offender into the community again.
- *Pre-emptive deterrence*, which involves deterring crime before it is committed.
- The *minimal use of incarceration*, given that prisons simply serve to create hardened, bitter criminals and diminished chances of "going straight."

As we will see, like the Young Offenders Act before it, the new Youth Criminal Justice Act contains the promise of demarginalizing and diverting young offenders through the provision of Extrajudicial Measures. Thus, there is a possibility that the existing legislative framework, if implemented properly, could be effective in reducing crime. By removing young offenders from the court process and at the same time allowing them to confront their behaviour in the presence of a victim, we may be able to return some power to control the situation to the actors involved while reducing the costs of processing through the criminal justice system (Alvi 1986).

The question remains, however, as to whether there is any real political will to create environments that reduce inequality, relative deprivation, and discontent.

References

Alvi S (1986) Realistic crime prevention strategies through alternative measures for youth. In: Currie D, MacLean BD (eds) The administration of justice, Social Research Unit, Department of Sociology, University of Saskatchewan, Saskatoon, pp 112–127

Berger P, Luckmann T (1967) The social construction of reality. Anchor, New York

Currie E (2004) The road to whatever: middle-class culture and the crisis of adolescence. Henry Holt, New York

Muncie J (2008) The "punitive turn" in juvenile justice: cultures of control and rights compliance in western Europe and the USA. Youth Justice 8(2):107–121

Contents

Chapter 1
The Criminalization and Control of Youth in Canada: A History

Abstract This chapter provides a historical summary of key legislation supporting societal responses to youth crime in Canada. It highlights the changing nature of perceptions of youth over time, and the contemporary emphasis on the rights of society and individual responsibility. Specifically, the history of youth crime legislation in Canada reflects a gradual shift away from the attitude that children were no different than adults, through a period where children were seen as in need of protection and welfare, to a situation today which attempts to balance the rights of society with those of the young offender while recognizing, in principle, that the root causes of much crime are social. Increasingly, however, we may be witnessing a transition in youth crime legislation reflecting a "get tough" punishment oriented ethos, at the same time, paradoxically, as we are embracing the idea of "getting tough" on the causes of crime.

I was born in England, and grew up in Glasgow, Scotland till the age of 12, when my family emigrated to Canada. As a young boy of South Asian descent, with Muslim parents, I arrived in Saskatoon, Saskatchewan with a thick Scottish accent, brown skin and a religious-cultural heritage that had already shaped me in many ways. In the context of the almost completely Anglo-white prairies of the early 1970s, I must have appeared to many of my hosts to be a strange bird indeed. I existed in a state of liminality for many years—a state of "in betweenness"—in that I was neither Canadian (yet) nor Scottish, nor South Asian. Fortunately, like all of my peers and friends, I was also a preadolescent, which meant that at least I shared a different but common type of liminal experience as neither a "child" anymore, nor an adult. Like other kids in that stage of life, I faced the challenges of negotiating various scripts for performing gender, for becoming a mature young adult, and taking my place in society as a productive citizen; all messages that have been transmitted and reproduced in various forms for generations (Purkayastha 2000). My generation, like all others, existed in relation to a set of cultural and structural codes, rules, and instructions that shaped our identities and provided the walls of the "boxes" into which we were told to fit, with often serious

S. Alvi, *Youth Criminal Justice Policy in Canada*, SpringerBriefs in Criminology,
DOI: 10.1007/978-1-4419-0273-3_1, © The Author(s) 2012

consequences if we had the temerity to break out of those boxes, or the misfortune to be labeled as misfits. In time, I was able to make the transition to adulthood relatively painlessly, thanks to the help of family, friends, school teachers, many mentors, and the fact that I was able to make reasonably good choices in an economic environment that did not displace me into a cycle of poverty.

Yet the transition to adulthood can be far more difficult for many adolescents, because the contours of the shift from childhood to adulthood depend greatly on the historical context and material circumstances in which youth grow up. The context in which I grew up was one of post-war prosperity, followed closely by economic crises, important cultural shifts and attendant movements in policies and practices of childrearing, and social control.

Recently, some scholars have argued that today's material circumstances are much different than those experienced by previous generations. They couch their arguments within debates around the emergence, variously, of *post-industrial, post-modern,* or *late-modern,* societies in the West. One of the central claims of this perspective is that something important has been lost in today's society, including connections to "community," salubrious ties between individuals, vanishing family values, and a range of other laments superceded by technologically driven, mass produced and hyper-individuated social relations (Beck 1992). Giroux (2009) for instance, argues that today's "youth crime complex" is a direct consequence of the gradual but important demise of collective supports in modern societies such as Canada, as demonstrated in institutions such as schools, the family, the state and other civic institutions. Similarly, Muncie (2008, p. 108, 2009) maintains that the rise of harsh, correctional, and punitive policies towards youth transgressions are occurring in a context in which historical protections afforded to youth have been "rapidly dissolving." Still others have argued that despite historic rights guaranteed by the UN Convention on the Rights of the Child, more young people than ever before are falling through the cracks in the economic and social fabrics of both developed and developing societies. These viewpoints, then, emphasize that there are some things that are both qualitatively and quantitatively different today from preceding eras that warrant scholarly consideration.

To shed some light on this claim, this chapter traces the historical trajectories of young people's relationship to the society in which they live. It does so as a prelude to a central argument that will be maintained in this book, namely, that the control and containment of youth in general, and young offenders in particular, cannot be reduced to a focus on the personal or individual characteristics of young people. Nor, indeed, should control of youth necessarily be seen as the panacea for youth offending. Rather, as Cullen et al. (1999, p. 190) and his colleagues have pointed out, crime "is best addressed not through greater amounts of control but by increasing social support." Before we delve into this argument, however, it is important to clarify what we mean by "youth," because there are important legal issues associated with the definition of youth, including: At what age can we reasonably expect that young people will understand the consequences of their actions? To what extent can youth be said to understand their legal rights and obligations? When can we reasonably compare the knowledge and "morality" of a young person to that of an adult? Clearly, these are not easy questions (Peterson-Badali et al. 1997).

Defining Youth

The definition of a young offender is inextricably tied to the definition of what constitutes childhood and adolescence. Most of us believe that there is nothing inherently difficult about defining what it is to be "young," and what it means to "offend," and that therefore, a young offender is simply a person between the ages of 12 and 17 who has broken a law. This is precisely how young offenders are defined using current conventional *legalistic definitions* of youth as laid out in the Youth Criminal Justice Act (YCJA). However, upon closer scrutiny the definition of what constitutes a youth is by no means as simple or straightforward as it appears to be.

Think of the implications of the word "young" for a moment. Though I am approaching what some call "middle age," a friend of mine is fond of consoling me by asking "how old would you be if you didn't know how old you are?" His question prompts us to ask whether being young is a matter of how old we *think* we ought to act (you are as young as you feel) or whether it is simply a case of somehow objectively deciding that people who are say, under 18, are to be defined as "young." In fact, defining the "young person" is intimately related to the expectations we have of youth, and the consequences they may face when they do not meet these expectations. Given that expectations tend to change over time, it is not surprising, then, that the concepts of "childhood," "adolescence" and young persons" have meant different things at different times to different cultures (Caputo and Goldenberg 1986; Currie 1986; Albanese 2009).

Indeed, a great deal has been written around the definition of youth and children. One of the earliest scholars to problematize the notion of youth was the historian Aries (1962), whose central contribution was the idea that childhood is a "social construction." Drawing upon his analysis of the content of medieval portraits of families and children which portrayed youth as "miniature adults," Ariès concluded that the idea of childhood did not exist in medieval society. Indeed, as soon as children were able to survive without the assistance of their mothers or nannies, they would automatically be seen as adults. Although his work has been widely criticized on methodological grounds (See Hendrick 1992), Ariès' work alerted scholars to the possibility that childhood is not a "natural" condition, but in fact is a construction linked to the cultural and social conditions of a given time period.

Prior to these insights, most definitions and by extension, expectations of young people were rooted in developmental perspectives. In these approaches, childhood, youth, or adolescence are defined in relation to the development of the human body or mind. Young people go through periods of intense and rapid psychological and physiological changes and it is these changes that are responsible for behavioural and attitudinal shifts. The earliest proponent of this view was Hall (1904), who argued that the period of adolescence is characterized by "storm and stress" and was predicated on evolutionary (and therefore natural) processes. Thus, all adolescents would inevitably go through periods of turmoil and emotional instability. There was nothing, in Hall's opinion, that adults could do about this except to "stand back and let the processes see themselves through according to their inherent evolutionary logic." (Côté and Allahar 2006, p. 16).

There are also sociological developmental perspectives that focus on the ways in which adults interact with adolescents which in turn can result in negative consequences. For example, Agnew (2003, p. 263) has argued that the peak in youthful offending which appears to be invariant across cultures may be related to the fact that young people are accorded some, but not all of the privileges of adulthood, which in turn results in certain factors that are related to offending, such as reduced supervision, increasing social and academic demands, increased demand for adult privileges and a reduction in the ability to cope in a legitimate manner. As Albanese (2009, p. 19) points out, these "ages and stages" approaches are increasingly being challenged by new developments in the sociology of childhood that focus on children as "'being' and doing, rather than a category of people being acted upon or 'becoming'."

In this short volume I adopt the latter approach, focusing on the importance of understanding that children are perfectly capable of participating in social life. Children possess and exert agency, and should not be seen as an "incomplete" other category of human existence or the passive recipients of adult socialization. As such, the notions of childhood and youth are not only social constructions, they are, as Heywood (2001) points out, also variables in the same sense as race, class and gender exhibit variation across and within societies. Thus, life for a middle class, white male youth in Canada is very different from the life experiences of a female, Aboriginal youth growing up in an inner city neighbourhood. I do not deny the important influence of biology and psychology in taking this stance, but as I will try to demonstrate it is critical that we understand young people's experiences in terms of the ways that biological and psychological developments intersect and are braided with social and cultural forces. This stance also helps to avoid potential problems that may arise if we mischaracterize youth as having enough agency to always make responsible decisions. As I will argue later, such a representation may lend itself well to contemporary legal and social tendencies in Canada and elsewhere to "responsibilize" children and youth—a perspective holding that if children are capable of acting then surely they can be held responsible for their actions. Thus, if the child can be conceptualized as being rational, he or she is also subject to the logics of deterrence theory which posits the rational choice offender and attempts to deter crime by making examples of the offender (general deterrence), or by protecting the public from offenders by incarcerating them (specific deterrence).

However, while it is important to conceptualize children as having agency, it is quite another to assume that children's actions are always rational, or that they should meet a standard of behaviour that we would expect of adults. And this is particularly true when we consider that actions and choices are conditioned by the social and cultural conditions in which they are made. Thus, while this volume focuses on the formal and informal control of youth as demarcated by legalistic definitions, it is important to remember that legal definitions sit in uneasy tension with recent scholarship on what it means to be a young person. If the concept of "youth" is contentious, so is the concept of "youth offender."

Controlling Young People in Canada: The Pre-legal Era

I have suggested that just as young people are affected by the social and economic conditions in which they live, so too are they affected by the laws and criminal justice policies that exist at any given time. Put differently, the ways in which we act both informally (for example in everyday life) and formally (legally) towards each at any given time depends greatly on the norms, values, political and economic conditions that exist in a given era. There was a time in Canada in which young people were regulated by informal norms rather than formal laws. In this "pre-legal" era, which I define as the time between pioneer settlement and the emergence of the Juvenile Delinquent Act of 1908, the discipline and control of children was strongly associated with the fact that there were few laws to speak of, though there had been occasional proposals to fine or punish the parents of recalcitrant youth, calls for military justice and more garrison troops in various settlements (Bell 2007, p. 14).

Many of the children of the earliest Canadian pioneers were considered assets, were treasured and valued by their parents and the community, and, with the exception of Aboriginal children who were beginning to suffer a long period of institutionalized abuse at this time (Eisler and Schissel 2008), were even indulged. The relatively lawless environment of this era meant that there were plenty of opportunities for offending, yet historians have argued that parental overindulgence was often blamed when young people offended (Bell 2007). In his excellent history of juvenile delinquency in Canada, Carrigan (1998, pp. 4–25) points out that in the late eighteenth century, the children who were at risk of criminal behaviour tended to be those who had been neglected or abandoned, particularly those who lived in settlements with military garrisons. Other children lived in poverty-stricken families suffering attendant sickness and disease which in turn contributed to becoming orphaned. The fur trade offered opportunities not only for young people to make a living, but also a lawless environment filled with temptation. Moreover, delinquents were capable of committing a range of petty offences, including "violations of local ordinances, nuisance offences, vandalism, petty theft, and breaches of the moral laws" (Carrigan 1998, p. 25), as well as serious ones. Offenders also came from both urban and rural backgrounds. As it is today, boys committed more offences than girls. Punishment could be minor or severe, and it was not unusual for youth caught violating some moral or formal law to be whipped, incarcerated in work houses, detained in jail indefinitely, held in custody until their parents paid a fine, or even hanged. In addition, children could be punished even if they were considered to have the *potential* of committing a crime (Schissel 1993). Girls were often punished for vices and immoralities including prostitution and infanticide and were often incarcerated with boys or adults.

All of these realities paint a fairly grim picture of what it was like to be a young person who did not belong to a family that was willing and able to provide proper care for the child. As Carrigan (1998, p. 26) notes, at this moment in Canadian history, "The one common denominator that many young offenders shared was parental neglect."

The Era of the Juvenile Delinquent

The situation for youth in conflict with the law began to change with the gradual influx of immigrant European children which had spanned the late seventeenth and nineteenth centuries. Indeed, according to Neff (2000), between 1869 and 1925 more than 80,000 dependent children emigrated from Britain to Canada. These often parentless and destitute children came to fulfill the function of serving the rich or providing cheap labour as field workers, or for an emerging class of industrializing entrepreneurs. As many of them were also considered to be "homeless waifs," "street urchins" or were thought to be from questionable backgrounds, they tended to be blamed for the majority of youth deviance in this era (Schissel 1993, pp. 8–9; West 1984). In effect, the children receiving the bulk of attention from the criminal justice system continued to be the poor and neglected. They were viewed as "problem children" (Currie 1986), and many of them were placed in private homes and required to receive an education, or in temporary institutions while they awaited placement in such homes. In fact, such orphan homes were regarded as reformatories that would ameliorate the problem of serious youth crime (Neff 2004, p. 3).

Interestingly, the behaviour of young people in conflict with the law was also seen to emanate from the inadequacies of their parents and families, particularly mothers. During this era, Canadians saw a transformation of the family unit which reflected the rapidly urbanizing and industrial nature of their society. Families became smaller, more mobile, and according to some commentators, internally mirrored the exploitative relationships characterizing capitalist economies (Barrett and McIntosh 1982; Alvi 1986; Currie 1986). Families began to be seen as central to the socialization and control of children who would have to take their place in a society that was no longer agricultural and rural and in which close kinship ties were eroding. The prevailing Victorian world view was premised on the ideas of "continuity, stability, and 'progress' as pathways of ongoing human development," (Comacchio 2006, p. 13), and, while there was also tacit acknowledgement of the problem of child poverty, there was greater concern that such children lacked morality primarily because parents had failed to bring them up properly (Houston 1972).

In addition, since education was seen as one way to deal with the problem of delinquency, and because the economy required trained and skilled labourers, compulsory schooling also came to be seen as a major player in the "proper" development and socialization of children. It is in this era, then, that adolescence came to be viewed as a period of "innocence" in which the child would *delay* entrance into the labour market by receiving compulsory education in the context of a nurturing family environment (Currie 1986). A "child saving movement" composed largely of middle class women, argued that the justice system of the past could not preserve this state of innocence because it assumed that children's and adult's behaviour were essentially the same, and that therefore state and professional intervention was required (Platt 1977). Only children under seven were considered to be incapable of understanding right from wrong, and while those between the ages of seven and fourteen could sometimes raise a defence of *doli inapax* (incapacity to do wrong), essentially, criminal liability began at the age of seven (Bala 1997).

Another critical development that essentially coincided with calls for reform was the rise of "expertise" crystallized in the newly professionalizing fields of medicine, criminology, psychiatry and psychology. Within our understanding of crime, *positivist* criminology, which emphasized the role of social factors in causing crime, began to be preferred over the arguments that had previously been advanced in the field of classical criminology. Thus, while classical criminology saw crime as a consequence of "bad decision-making," positivist criminologists argued that social-structural factors were to blame. Physicians began to argue that while mothers and families were responsible for a child's wellbeing, it was important for communities to take responsibility as well, a transition that one scholar has termed the rise of the "public" child "constructed through medical discourses of protection, prevention, and statistical attention" (Gleason 2005, p. 231).

Accordingly, people came to believe that if a child committed a crime, responsibility for the child's condition should be laid on the family unit (and more often than not, mothers) and the school. The emphasis on the family as the core institution responsible for the care and upbringing of children underpinned a strategy of ensuring that both successful and problematic families should be provided with supports such as public, compulsory education, the creation of parks and recreation spaces, regulation of child labour and a campaign for worker's compensation (Sutherland 2000, p. 93). More particularly, many felt that it was lower class families that tended to fail, and thus any reform of the justice system for children should provide alternatives that fit more closely with an emerging "middle class" ideal of the family. Essentially, the idea was that youth should be accorded special treatment. New legislation in line with these new perspectives on the role and nature of youth was needed.

The first formal legislation enacted to address the new perspective on youth was entitled *An Act for the More Speedy Trial and Punishment of Juvenile Offenders* (1857). Its general intent was to accelerate the trial process for juvenile delinquents and to reduce the probability of a lengthy spell in jail before trial. A juvenile delinquent was defined as a person under the age of 16 who had committed an offence, and sentencing consisted of either imprisonment in a common jail or correctional house, either with or without hard labour for no longer than 3 months, or a fine not to exceed £5. As well, the accused could be ordered to restore any stolen property or pay the equivalent compensation (Gagnon 1984, pp. 21–22).

Québec was the first province to add, in 1869, a new sentencing provision that reflected a newfound emphasis on correction through proper schooling. In addition to the 3 month sentence, Québec changed their legislation to abolish hard labour while including a mandatory 2–5 year term in a certified Reformatory School *after* a jail sentence had been served.

According to Gagnon (1984), by 1894, the following principles regarding juvenile delinquents had become entrenched: They were to be kept separate from adult offenders at all stages of the criminal justice process. Instead of imprisonment, juvenile delinquents were to be sent to certified industrial schools, a children's aid society or a home for neglected children, where they could be "taught to lead useful lives."

By 1908, the passage of the *Act Respecting Juvenile Delinquents* (which later became the *Juvenile Delinquents Act*), represented a solidified philosophy of aid and protection for juvenile delinquents which located the causes of delinquency in the child's environment, and maintained that the solution to youth crime was to have the state take the place of the (incompetent) parent. In effect, it was assumed that if parents could not do the job of controlling and properly socializing their children, the state would have to intervene as a "kindly parent"—a principle which was called *parens patriae*.[1]

The outcome of this philosophy was that judges were directed to treat children not as criminals but as "misdirected and misguided" children requiring "aid, encouragement, help and assistance." (Juvenile Delinquents Act, s. 38). The following points summarize the key principles of the Act (Alvi 1986).

A juvenile delinquent was defined as "any child who violates an Provision of the Criminal Code, federal or provincial statute, municipal ordinance or by-law, or who is guilty of 'sexual immorality' or of similar vice, or who is liable for any other reason to be committed to an industrial school or reformatory"(s. 21).

The proceedings were to be as informal as possible and "consistent with a due regard for a proper administration of justice" (s. 17.1).

A child adjudged to be a juvenile delinquent would be subject to one or more of the following dispositions (outcomes):

Suspension of the Disposition
Adjournment of the hearing or disposition of the case for any definite or indefinite period

---

[1]   Actually, the term parens patriae translates to "father of the country," or "parent of the state," but the term essentially means that the state should act as a wise, kind but stern father.

A fine not to exceed $25

Commission of the child to the custody of a probation officer or any other suitable person

The child could be allowed to remain at home, subject to the visitation of a probation officer, with the child having to report to the probation officer or court as often as required

The child could be placed in a suitable family home as a foster home, subject to the friendly supervision of a probation officer and the further order of the court

The court could impose further or other conditions as may be deemed advisable

The child could be committed to the care of any children's aid society which must be approved by the legislature of the province and approved by the Lieutenant Governor in council, or, any municipality in which there is no children's aid society, to the care of the Superintendent if there is one, or;

The child could be committed to an industrial school, duly approved by the Lieutenant Governor in council (s. 20).

The legislation was based on a commitment to the therapeutic treatment of the juvenile delinquent, as illustrated by the following quotation: "where a child is adjudged to have committed a delinquency, he shall be dealt with not as an offender, but as one in a condition of delinquency, and therefore requiring help and guidance and proper supervision." The emphasis was on treatment provided by professional social workers who were to aid families perceived to be lacking in supervisory skills.

In many ways, the Juvenile Delinquents Act represented a fundamental shift away from prior approaches to juvenile justice which tended to view youth and adult behaviour as the same. But although there was now a more formal Act in place to address the uniqueness of the young person, much of its humanitarian potential was undermined by the fact that the language was vague, it lacked a guarantee of due process, still included a very wide range of "status" offences, and still allowed judges to invoke an extraordinarily wide range of dispositions (West 1984).

More specifically, problems with the Juvenile Delinquents Act included the following (Bala 1997):

Due process, such as the right to legal representation, tended to be inconsistently applied in different jurisdictions

Gender Bias: female adolescents, but not males, tended to be arrested for the vague offence of "sexual immorality," and typically, these girls came from socially disadvantaged backgrounds

Class bias: middle class children could be released to their parents, whereas immigrant and working class children received more severe punishment

In the 1980s it was discovered that many children had been abused while inmates in reformatory schools

Arbitrariness: there was a great deal of provincial variation with respect to age limits, access to legal services, and respect for legal rights, as well as in the use of diversion and custodial sentencing.

The Act seemed inadequate to meet new concerns around questions such as: Should the interests of the child be the *only* principle governing youth crime? Or, Why should the system be based on rehabilitation and not some other principle such as punishment and deterrence? The latter was particularly important in light of the apparent "failure" of rehabilitation programs.

Criminal justice officials such as police and judges had very broad powers to interpret the notion of "in the best interests of the child." This resulted in biased and inconsistent decision making.

During the first half of the 1900s, then, the Juvenile Delinquents Act provided the legal framework for youth in conflict with the law. The JDA was clearly an improvement over the unsystematic and often arbitrary treatment of delinquent youth in the pre-legal era. More broadly, however, the principles of the Act coincided with the responsibilization of parents, the rise of state power over children and families, and the medicalization of deviant behaviour. Gradually, delinquency came to be considered more of a disease than a social problem, while the unit of analysis gradually shifted to family and individuals and away from the social and structural environment. The JDA thus emphasized "therapeutic treatment," the important role of industrial schools and reformatories, and the expanding role of professional social-control agents such as probation officers and social workers. As Bala's summary of criticisms of the Act point out, too often it was the disadvantaged and poor who were singled out for these interventions (Alvi 2007). By the 1960s, enough questions and issues arose to warrant reconsideration of the legislation (Hylton 1994). Eventually, this dissatisfaction resulted in the development and implementation of new legislation—the Young Offenders Act.

The Young Offenders Act

Remarkably, it took nearly 75 years before the Juvenile Delinquents Act was replaced by a new set of principles to deal with youth crime contained within the Young Offenders Act. We have seen that much of the impetus for change was related to dissatisfaction with both basic principles and implementation of the JDA. But we must also consider the role of changing perceptions and realities of youth in the context of a changing Canadian culture and political economy.

For the most part, the Juvenile Delinquents Act remained in force with few major complaints from people until the 1960s. This is not surprising, given that this decade stands out as one of unprecedented social and cultural change, and, although it is difficult to say that such large scale changes were *responsible* for shifting attitudes and policies towards young offenders, we would be remiss in completely dismissing their influence (Corrado and Markwart 1992).

If we were to try and capture the tenor of the times in one word, we would probably be safe in calling this a "liberal" era. Attitudes towards war, for example shifted away from a hawkish, "get tough with everyone" approach towards a more conciliatory, peacemaking tone as the Vietnam war sensitized many to the problematic nature of US foreign policy and the ultimately destructive nature of war. Bob Dylan, John Lennon, and other folk and rock and roll musicians sang songs about peace, love and achieving higher consciousness through the use of drugs such as LSD, mescaline and marijuana. An attitude of "free love" seemed to be sweeping sexual consciousness, as many young people attempted to break free from what they perceived to be outmoded and traditional social norms and customs. Increasing attention was being paid to the problems of racism and racialization, and women's movements began to demand not only greater equality, but also offered scathing critiques of patriarchal social relations.

Indeed, we could also characterize this era as one which compelled many people to seek out new freedoms, experiment with alternative lifestyles, to problematize inequalities, and to turn attention to those less fortunate in society. In short, the 1960s spawned new concerns about the importance of equality in all facets of life, including the law, but at the same time, it provided people with a framework that would permit them to reexamine notions like "immorality," "gender," "class," and "race." Importantly, while many people were calling "traditional" social values into question, it was the youth who were at the center of change. Indeed, some commentators such as Bala (1997) have argued that the Young Offenders Act was the expression of "anti-youth sentiment," in that those youth were less likely to respect adult conventions of dress, taste, style and attitudes, were more individualistic, and less likely to show respect for authority. Not surprisingly, adult reactions to such political and cultural shifts often reflected the desire to return to "basic values," and an impetus towards conformity.

Economic change was also important in creating the conditions for the transformation of juvenile justice. The post-war period was very prosperous, with average family incomes (adjusted for inflation) increasing from $22,401 in 1951 to $50,208 in 1975 (Canadian Council on Social Development 2011), and, as many people enjoyed greater comforts and job security, they seemed more willing to look at those less fortunate than themselves. As Young (2007, p. 1) describes it, this "high modern" period was characterized by "the stolid, weighty, secure situations of Fordism, undergirded by the stable structures of family, marriage, and community (and) presented a taken for granted world of stasis and seeming permanency."

In Canada, changing attitudes towards the role of the welfare state manifested themselves in several major social policy changes. For instance, socialized health care or Medicare as it came to be called, began to be implemented in the early 1960s, and was a national program by the early 1970s. The federal Unemployment Insurance Act was reformed in 1955 and 1971, and the Canada Pension Plan Act was introduced in 1966. The ideas underpinning each of these important programs had to do with a philosophy of equality and help for those who had "fallen through the cracks" of an economic system whose fruits most people enjoyed. Finally, The Canadian Charter of Rights and Freedoms, implemented in 1982, provided a new framework for interpreting the rights and responsibilities of Canadians. Among other freedoms, it guaranteed a host of legal rights including equal treatment under the law, the right to legal counsel and the right not to be subjected to cruel and unusual punishment. Given these new rights, it is likely that the JDA could not have withstood legal challenges under the Charter (Hylton 1994). It was within the context of this emerging "liberal" ideology that Canadian policy makers began to question the relevance of the Juvenile Delinquents Act.

After much extended debate over the problems with the Juvenile Delinquents Act discussed in the preceding section, the Federal Committee on Juvenile Delinquency in Canada concluded in 1965 that the legislation had to be changed. Three separate bills followed the decision to replace the JDA, and in 1984, the Young Offenders Act (YOA) became law. The general principles of the act are set out in Table 1.1.

The declaration of principle indicates that the Young Offenders Act was a "hybrid" of the Juvenile Delinquents Act and a new set of principles emphasizing the rights of society to protection from crime, the rights of accused young persons to fair, equitable and consistent justice, and the notion that young people should be held accountable for their actions, but not in the same way as adults. Moreover, the Act emphasized the efficient and equitable administration of justice, and, as McGuire (1997, p. 189) reminds us:

The Young Offenders Act provides instruction for criminal procedure and administration of dispositions relating to young persons. It is an offender management tool, not a crime prevention tool.

Thus, the Act stressed that a young person in conflict with the law is a criminal (albeit a "special kind" of criminal) and not a misguided child. At least on paper, the Young Offenders Act keeps the welfare approach to youth crime found in the Juvenile Delinquents Act, but also emphasizes law and order in a manner in keeping with the principle of "rights."

In addition to the focus on the efficient and egalitarian administration of justice, the Act included an important section allowing young people in conflict with the law to avoid the stigmatizing and potentially harmful effects of processing in the criminal justice system. Section 4, entitled *Alternative Measures*, maintained that whenever possible, young offenders should be diverted from the criminal justice system, as long as such diversion is consistent with the principle of protection of society (see Table 1.2). Youth participating in diversion programs might engage in a variety of activities such as reconciliation and restitution to the victim, performing services for the victim, an apology, or service to the community. As well, the provinces varied in their approach to the types of offences considered to be eligible for alternative measures, with some considering all offences and others excluding the more serious crimes such as murder and manslaughter.

The assumption behind alternative measures was that when young people go through the process of arrest, detention, court and sentencing, the very act of being labelled a "young offender" greatly contributes to the potential for those individuals to *see* themselves as young offenders. Thus, alternative measures exist to divert certain individuals away from the criminal justice system so that they do not "see themselves" as criminals and thus "become" criminals. In short, Section 4 in Table 1.2 provided the flexibility to divert young offenders from the criminal

Table 1.1 The young offenders act declaration of principle

Section 3

3. (1) It is hereby recognized and declared that

(a) crime prevention is essential to the long-term protection of society and requires addressing the underlying causes of crime by young persons and developing multi-disciplinary approaches to identifying and effectively responding to children and young persons at risk of committing offending behaviour in the future;

(a.1) while young persons should not in all instances be held accountable in the same manner or suffer the same consequences for their behaviour as adults, young persons who commit offences should nonetheless bear responsibility for their contraventions;

(b) society must, although it has the responsibility to take reasonable measures to prevent criminal conduct by young persons, be afforded the necessary protection from illegal behaviour;

(c) young persons who commit offences require supervision, discipline and control, but, because of their state of dependency and level of development and maturity, they also have special needs and require guidance and assistance;

(c.1) the protection of society, which is a primary objective of the criminal law applicable to youth, is best served by rehabilitation, wherever possible, of young persons who commit offences, and rehabilitation is best achieved by addressing the needs and circumstances of a young person that are relevant to the young person's offending behaviour;

(d) where it is not inconsistent with the protection of society, taking no measures or taking measures other than judicial proceedings under this Act should be considered for dealing with young persons who have committed offences;

(e) young persons have rights and freedoms in their own right, including those stated in the Canadian Charter of Rights and Freedoms or in the Canadian Bill of Rights, and in particular a right to be heard in the course of, and to participate in, the processes that lead to decisions that affect them, and young persons should have special guarantees of their rights and freedoms;

(f) in the application of this Act, the rights and freedoms of young persons include a right to the least possible interference with freedom that is consistent with the protection of society, having regard to the needs of young persons and the interests of their families;

(g) young persons have the right, in every instance where they have rights or freedoms that may be affected by this Act, to be informed as to what those rights and freedoms are; and

(h) parents have responsibility for the care and supervision of their children, and, for that reason, young persons should be removed from parental supervision either partly or entirely only when measures that provide for continuing parental supervision are inappropriate.

justice system while ensuring that the young offender accepts responsibility for the actions that are the basis of their offences.

Another important aspect of alternative measures was its emphasis on community delivery of programs (Wardell 1986). While it could be argued that this strategy is designed to have the community more involved with their children, it could also be suggested that community emphasis places the burden on the public to deal with the transgressions of their youth. Indeed, an important shortcoming of the alternative measures section was that it relied on the community to determine the level and kind of restitution that a young person should offer. This meant that the community would have to look for the appropriate resources to make these dispositions happen, but communities often do *not* have access to such

Table 1.2 The young offenders act, alternative measures

Section 4

4. (1) Alternative measures may be used to deal with a young person alleged to have committed an offence instead of judicial proceedings under this Act only if:

(a) the measures are part of a program of alternative measures authorized by the Attorney General or his delegate or authorized by a person, or a person within a class of persons, designated by the Lieutenant Governor in Council of a province;

(b) the person who is considering whether to use such measures is satisfied that they would be appropriate, having regard to the needs of the young person and the interests of society;

(c) the young person, having been informed of the alternative measures, fully and freely consents to participate therein;

(d) the young person has, before consenting to participate in the alternative measures, been advised of his right to be represented by counsel and been given a reasonable opportunity to consult with counsel;

(e) the young person accepts responsibility for the act or omission that forms the basis of the offence that he is alleged to have committed;

(f) there is, in the opinion of the Attorney General or his agent, sufficient evidence to proceed with the prosecution of the offence; and

(g) the prosecution of the offence is not in any way barred at law.

Restriction on use

(2) Alternative measures shall not be used to deal with a young person alleged to have committed an offence if the young person

(a) denies his participation or involvement in the commission of the offence; or

(b) expresses his wish to have any charge against him dealt with by the youth court.

Admissions not admissible in evidence

(3) No admission, confession or statement accepting responsibility for a given act or omission made by a young person alleged to have committed an offence as a condition of his being dealt with by alternative measures shall be admissible in evidence against him in any civil or criminal proceedings.

No bar to proceedings

(4) The use of alternative measures in respect of a young person alleged to have committed an offence is not a bar to proceedings against him under this Act, but

(a) where the youth court is satisfied on a balance of probabilities that the young person has totally complied with the terms and conditions of the alternative measures, the youth court shall dismiss any charge against him; and

(b) where the youth court is satisfied on a balance of probabilities that the young person has partially complied with the terms and conditions of the alternative measures, the youth court may dismiss any charge against him if, in the opinion of the court, the prosecution of the charge would, having regard to the circumstances, be unfair, and the youth court may consider the young person's performance with respect to the alternative measures before making a disposition under this Act.

Laying of information, etc.

(5) Subject to subsection (4), nothing in this section shall be construed to prevent any person from laying an information, obtaining the issue or confirmation of any process or proceeding with the prosecution of any offence in accordance with law.

resources. On the other hand, Wardell (1986) suggested that cost control was the real reason behind government's commitment to the principle of "non-intervention."

There were other criticisms of this section of the act. For instance, some maintained that using alternative measures was only slightly different than actually charging, processing and incarcerating young offenders. This argument, called "net-widening" suggests that placing youth in a diversion program merely substitutes one form of social control for another (Matthews 1979). Others, particularly those subscribing to the "law, order and justice" ideal that underpins the Young Offenders Act, argued that placing youth in a diversion program does not permit "real" justice to be done. Nevertheless, Statistics Canada reported that during 1997–1998 nearly 33,000 youth cases were subject to alternative measures (excluding British Columbia), that females were more likely to participate in alternative measures programs, that most (57%) cases involved theft under $5,000, and that the alternative measures programs were completed successfully by 89% of youth (Kowalski 1999).

On the whole, then, the YOA was a controversial piece of legislation (Corrado and Markwart 1994). Many conservative voices argued that the Act was not tough enough on young offenders, presumably because it permitted a maximum sentence of 3 years for crimes that would have resulted in a life sentence for adults, provided youth with "too many" rights, did not protect society from dangerous youth, and protected the anonymity of young offenders (Leschied and Gendreau 1994). These concerns, in turn, were being debated in a media environment in which youth crime was being sensationalized as "being out of control," a problem that was exacerbated by horrific, but rare cases such as the murder of Reena Virk in British Columbia, and the drive by shooting of Nicholas Battersby in Ottawa (Gabor 1999).

Others pointed out that while the highlighting of due process and youth rights was a good thing, the Act ignored the more fundamental cognitive, psychological and social functioning needs of adolescents, thereby signalling a shift in emphasis from therapy to social control (Awad 1987). In 1995, significant amendments were introduced to the YOA, most fundamentally in the declaration of principle which emphasized the rehabilitative ideal and protection of society (McGuire 1997). In addition, sentences for murder were increased, 16- and 17-year-olds could be transferred to adult court and those charged with minor offences were to enjoy the benefits of community-based rehabilitation strategies.

Regardless of these changes, public concern, fuelled by continued media amplification of the "youth crime problem," continued to drive the federal government's desire to amend or replace the YOA (see Table 1.3) equally important, was the continued drift in Canadian social and economic policy towards governance strategies that explicitly reject the welfare model. As Muncie (2006, p. 771) reminds us:

> The economic argument that the welfare sector is unproductive and parasitic of market capitalism has fed into a range of critiques of social governments as monopolistic, as overloaded and as failing to ameliorate social inequalities. Welfare practice and professionals have been attacked from all sides of the political spectrum as unaccountable, as overbearing and as destructive of other forms of support such as community and the family. Notions of social engineering, social solidarity, social benefits, social work, social

Table 1.3 Amendments to the young offenders act, 1986–1998

Year	Amendments
1986	Technical amendments to custody placements
1992	Increased maximum sentence from 3 to 5 years for murder
	Clarified rules for transferring youth to adult court
1995 Bill C.19	Increased maximum sentence to 10 years for murder
	Created presumption of transfer for 16 and 17 year olds charged with serious violent offences to adult court
	Allowed victim impact statements in court supported information sharing among youth justice professionals
1996 (August) Federal–Provincial–Territorial Task Force on Youth Justice Report	Review of the YOA
	Report referred to Standing Committee on Justice and Legal Affairs for consideration
1997 (April) Standing Committee on Justice and Legal Affairs Youth Justice Review Report	Review of the Youth Justice System
	14 recommendations
1997 (August) Meeting of First Ministers	With exception of Quebec, called for meaningful amendments to the YOA.
	Committed to improving preventative and rehabilitative programs for young offenders
1997 (December) Federal–Provincial–Territorial Meetings of Ministers Responsible for Justice	Proposed amendments to the YOA
1998 (May) Federal Youth Justice Strategy Announced	

Source Adapted from Dell, 1998

welfare, it is contended, have been largely dismantled to create the conditions for a responsible citizenship.

In spirit the YOA established that youth in conflict of the law had a special status, recognized the importance of due process, and sought to balance these principles with the rights of victims and the protection of society. On another level, the YOA was in force in a society that was gradually drifting towards a law and order mentality, while at the same time, deeper, structural problems in Canada, such as inequality, racism, sexism, and poverty, remained unexamined in relation to young people. Instead the system favoured a strategy that paid lip service to the possibilities inherent in alternative measures, overemphasized individual responsibilities and traits, and propelled the steady entrenchment of punishment and incarceration. By 1998, nearly three-quarters of cases heard in court under the YOA were for minor offences, and 75% of youth were sentenced to custody for minor offences (Doob and Sprott 2009). By the early part of the twenty first century, Canada had one of the lowest rates of diversion from the system, and one of the highest rates of youth custody in the world (Bala et al. 2009).

In a document entitled *A Strategy for the Renewal of Youth Justice* (1999), the federal government outlined three shortcomings of the YOA, as follows:

First, not enough is done to prevent troubled youth from entering a life of crime. Second, the system must improve the way it deals with the most serious, violent youth: not just in terms of sentencing but also in ensuring that these youth are provided with the intensive, long-term rehabilitation that is in their and society's interest. Third, the system relies too heavily on custody as a response to the vast majority of non-violent youth when alternative, community-based approaches can do a better a job of instilling social values such as responsibility and account-ability, helping to right wrongs and ensuring that valuable resources are targeted where they are most needed.

The Act was regarded as somewhat technically and procedurally deficient. For example, it could sometimes take years to "bump" young offenders to adult court. Moreover, the length of time between the commission of an offence and sen-tencing was often far too long. Hence, one set of recommendations stated that the act should be revised to make processing more efficient and timely, and that criminal justice officials should be given the power to exercise more discretion.

Another important recommendation was centred on the recognition that effectively addressing youth crime requires dealing with the root causes of delinquency. It had been argued that the way to do this was through community-based crime prevention and by addressing "the social conditions" associated with these root causes. In effect, this represented an attempt, on paper at least, to strengthen the effectiveness and reemphasize the potential of alternative measures, while at the same time focusing on the lack of social and economic resources facing many youth.

There was also a perception that the Act did not address a perceived increase in violent crime, and could not deal effectively with repeat young offenders. This prompted an emphasis on "firm measures." Generally, this strategy was in keeping with amendments which increased the length of sentences for murder. Moreover, it reinforced the idea that society should send a strong message to those who commit the most dangerous offences, and that young people need to be held accountable and responsible for their actions. In this way, it was presumed that other young people will be deterred from committing crimes. Another expression of this "deterrence" strategy is found in the proposal for the publication of the names of young offenders who receive an adult sentence or who commit serious crimes (i.e., murder, attempted murder, manslaughter, aggravated sexual assault and any offence which forms part of a pattern of serious violent offences). One M.P. Jack Ramsay of the former Reform Party of Canada proposed An Act to amend the Young Offenders Act, recommending transferring older offenders who commit violent offences to adult court, *limiting* the application of alternative measures, designating certain young offenders as "dangerous offenders," establishing public safety as a *dominant* consideration in the application of the law respecting young offenders, and *removing* privacy provisions.

In addition, based on the idea that the vast majority of young offenders can become law-abiding citizens, the Youth Justice Strategy emphasized rehabilitation and reintegration of the young offender and called for increased participation in the youth criminal justice system from parents, victims and the community. Although the Young Offenders Act already made provisions for parental rights, there was some discussion over the need to make parents more accountable and responsible for their children. In addition, it was argued that the role of victims of youth crime needs to be enhanced, particularly with respect to the impact of the crime, compensation, and the benefits youth might accrue by confronting the harms they caused.

Lastly, there were calls for more community participation, especially with respect to the role of Youth Justice Committees which would coordinate and deliver services to youth in conflict with the law under Section 4 in Table 1.2 (Alternative Measures) of the Act.

The Youth Criminal Justice Act

In the late 1990s Canadians began to discuss the ramifications of a reform and partial reconceptualization of young offenders and the law. The new legislation, the YCJA, which went into effect in April 2003, is a blend of strategies such as the cost-effective management of "risky children," a lowering of the age at which a youth may be imprisoned in adult facilities, and a focus on creating "meaningful consequences" for youth. In theory, then, the new Act signifies a concern for the welfare of young people, coupled with the crystallization in law of a crime-control ideology.

The Justice Minister at the time, Anne McLellan argued that the new legislation would emphasize preventative measures, while at the same time reassuring Canadians that the law would be tough on serious youth offenders (See Box 1.1).

Thus, the Act combines "meaningful consequences" for youth offenders with an emphasis on addressing the social circumstances that underpin offending, recognition that youth are not a homogeneous category, rehabilitation and reintegration into society, concern for the rights of victims, and protection of the public. Moreover, the Act represents "an astute political compromise" because it "gets tough" on serious offending while reducing reliance on incarceration thereby ostensibly restoring public confidence in the youth justice system (Bala et al. 2009).

The YCJA takes a progressively tougher approach to youth offending. The first part is devoted to "extra-judicial measures" where, if the offence is deemed to be minor, youth are encouraged to "acknowledge and repair the harm caused to the victim and the community, and to encourage families and victims to be involved in designing and implementing appropriate measures" (Bala et al. 2009). The next section, extra-judicial sanctions, replaces Section 4 (Alternative Measures) in Table 1.2 that existed under the YOA. It is essentially based on the same idea as Alternative Measures; that diverting youth from the criminal justice system is appropriate when the offence committed is minor. However, under extra-judicial sanctions, the youth will have a record that can later be taken into account in subsequent court hearings. Subsequent sections of the Act lay out procedures for youth who are charged and must appear in court, as well as sentencing provisions.

However, one of the problems with this interpretation is that it contradicts another principle of the act, namely; deterrence. On the one hand we have the recognition that processing individuals through the criminal justice system can have negative consequences in that it "amplifies tendencies on the part of the young person to commit offences" (Doob and Cesaroni 2004, p. 42). On the other hand we have the idea that processing youth will have a deterrent effect on young offenders and the tacit acceptance of the idea that punishment works.

Given that these two objectives are somewhat at odds, they illustrate one way in which the YCJA tries to be "all things to all people" (Barber and Doob 2004).

While the Act is clear about the importance of the long-term protection of society from youth crime, it also is very clear about the importance of rehabilitation, and relatedly, the limited use of incarceration. Nearly a decade after the implementation of the Act, there is some good evidence to suggest that the latter goal is being met. Between 2002/2003 and 2008, youth court caseloads have decreased by 26%, which can be attributed to a decrease in charges laid by police (Tustin and Lutes 2008, p. 7). The YCJA has a strict provision (s. 29.1) that prohibits judges from remanding youth to custody prior to sentencing as a "substitute for appropriate child protection, mental health or other social measures." As Bala and his colleagues point out, however, it is difficult to know the impact of the YCJA on youth in remand custody because there are no data available for Ontario prior to 2003/4, the province which accounts for almost half the national total of remand in custody cases (Bala et al. 2009, p. 140). There is also some indication that judges are crafting sentences that are more proportional to the nature of the offence and the offenders degree of responsibility for that offence (Pulis and Sprott 2005).

Thus, there is provisional evidence that the Act is working as intended, at least with respect to reducing incarceration rates and the use of remand. But with respect to the other stated intentions of the Act—rehabilitation of the offender, and attending to the causes of youth offending, there are most certainly fewer positive things to say, a point I will take up in more detail in the next chapter. In part, the criminal justice system may not be to blame for its lack of effectiveness regarding rehabilitation and attention to the underlying causes of youth offending because it encourages "the community" and the victim to take an active role in "making a young person accountable for his or her criminal behaviour" (Tustin and Lutes 2008, p. 3). As I have argued elsewhere (Alvi 2007), we cannot rely on laws to prevent crime because laws are post-hoc. Accordingly, attention to the social and cultural problems that condition youth crime are social justice, not criminal justice issues.

Such social justice issues exist, I would argue, in dynamic tension with social forces that are committed to preserving the status quo, or even taking us back to less progressive social relations. An important and ongoing example of this argument can be found by examining proposed amendments to the YCJA, represented in Bill C-4, which was dropped from discussion due to the dissolution of the Canadian government in April 2011, but, as of the reelection of a majority Conservative government on May 2, 2011, is likely to reapper as part of a comprehensive crime bill. The bill's contents indicate that the current government, along with many interest groups, is bent on making the Act, yet again, "tougher on crime."

In 2006, the Nunn Commission, upon which Bill C-4 recommendations are based, advocated that the clause "long-term protection of the public" in the current YCJA be replaced by the clauses "protecting the public" (which could be interpreted as the long *and* short terms)" (Casavant and Valiquet 2010, p. 8). Bill C-4 (also known as *Sébastien's Law-Protecting the public from Violent Young offenders)* lays out the following proposed amendments (Casavant and Valiquet 2010, p. 1):

- establishes deterrence and denunciation as sentencing principles similar to the principles provided in the adult criminal justice system (clause 7);
- expands the case law definition of a violent offence to include reckless behaviour endangering public safety (clause 2);
- amends the rules for pre-sentence detention (also called "pre-trial detention") to facilitate the detention of young persons accused of crimes against property punishable by a maximum term of 5 years or more (clause 4);
- authorizes the court to impose a prison sentence on a young person who has previously been subject to a number of extrajudicial sanctions (clause 8);
- requires the Crown to consider the possibility of seeking an adult sentence for young offenders 14–17 years of age convicted of murder, attempted murder, manslaughter or aggravated sexual assault (clauses 11 and 18);
- facilitates publication of the names of young offenders convicted of violent offences (clauses 20 and 24);
- requires police to keep a record of any extrajudicial measures imposed on young persons so that their criminal tendencies can be documented (clause 25);
- prohibits the imprisonment of young persons in adult correctional facilities (clause 21).

There have been numerous criticisms levelled at Bill C-4 and there are likely to be others depending on whether the Bill is reintroduced to Parliament and the form it may take after a new government is elected. However, I want to draw attention to several issues in the Bill that reflect, in my view, a broader set of trends in youth criminal justice policy. First, and as noted above, the Bill shifts attention to both the long *and* short term protection of the public, and also establishes the principles of deterrence and denunciation. These principles, if adopted, leave open the possibility that the emphasis in the YCJA will shift away from rehabilitation towards deterrence principles, which in turn, assume that young people are capable of making rational choices by weighing the costs and benefits of their actions, and that locking them up to make an example of them (general deterrence) while at the same time protecting the public (specific deterrence), actually works as a sentencing principle, which it does not (Canadian Bar Association 2010).

Second, the amendment to broaden the definition of a violent offence to include reckless behaviour that could "create a substantial likelihood of causing bodily harm" is very vague and opens the possibility that youth committing an offence that *might* have resulted in bodily harm could be imprisoned for five or more years.

Third, the Bill proposes that police should keep records of any extrajudicial measures that have been imposed on the youth, so that their "criminal tendencies" can be documented, and so that judges can consider such patterns in sentencing deliberations. Not only does this proposal diminish police discretion, it also assumes that such alleged "tendencies" can not only be understood but accurately observed. Equally important, it turns the attention of the public and the criminal justice system towards the behaviour of individuals, rather than the ways in which behaviours are connected with social systems and experiences (Canadian Bar Association 2010).

From my perspective, what is interesting about the sentiments expressed in Bill C-4 is its' "punitive turn," (Muncie 2008) characterized by a preoccupation with principles that were abandoned years ago, and a punishment ethos that has been discredited in the social scientific and criminological literature. Central to this development is a growing reliance on the "criminology of the dangerous other" in which youth (as well as women, the poor, and particular racial/ethnic groups) are singled out as the category considered most risky and in need of control (Garland 2001).

In Ontario, for instance, Conservative Premier Mike Harris began his tenure in 1995 by waging a campaign to discipline particular categories of youth, most notably "squeegee kids," whose only "crime" appeared to be that of attempting to make a living in an economy that has consistently denied them legitimate opportunities. Moreover, in the two decades prior to Harris's term in office, youth unemployment rates in Canada rose from 14% in 1980 to 18% in 1995 for those completing high school, and more and more youth were working part-time in low-paying, service sector jobs with little chance of advancement, minimal training for more advanced jobs, and reduced or non-existent benefits (Health Canada 1999). Not much has changed in the decade and a half since Harris's disciplinary tactics. Like their historical counterparts, modern Canadians are being subject to a discourse of children, "the nuisances that they can pose, and the more serious disruption that they can auger" (Foster 2009, p. 213). Now, as then, they are seen as morally deficient, lazy, increasingly violent, except that the focus now is also on racialized youth and the false specter of "increasingly violent girls."

These shifts have occurred in the context of transformations in our market-based society that paradoxically rely on youth to consume goods and services but at the same time systematically exclude large segments of them from participation in worthwhile, remunerative work, and as we shall see, subject them to responsibilization strategies in a zero-tolerance environment (Currie 2004).

Indeed, today's youth are increasingly forced into a "prolonged state of social marginality' (Petersen and Mortimer 1994), given the rapid decline of decent work opportunities for young people—and in particular for those who come from poor or dispossessed backgrounds. At the same time, and perhaps more than ever, young people are subjected to a market orientation in which consumption is depicted as "an end in itself and as a measure of social status and human value" (Caston 1998). Thus we are now in an era in which more and more youth are experiencing deprivation relative to other people's children, demonization, and fewer opportunities to attain the "glittering prizes" of capitalism through legitimate means (Young 1999).

In democracies, and in principle, law is supposed reflect the interests of the majority, who, we can presume from looking at recent developments, seem to think that youth crime is enough of a problem to warrant harsher, more exacting penalties. This begs the questions: Who are these youth and what crimes are they really committing? And what is the nature of the underlying circumstances in which they exist? In the next chapter we turn our attention to the issue of determining the characteristics of young offenders, the nature and amount of youth crime in Canada, and the social milieu in which young people live.

Box 1.1. Youth Crime Law is History: New Legislation will be Tougher on Violent Young Offenders

Stephen Bindman and Jim Bronskill

Tuesday 28 April 1998

The Ottawa Citizen

The federal government plans to replace the much-maligned Young Offenders Act to signal a new approach to dealing with youth crime, the Citizen has learned.

Justice Minister Anne McLellan's long-awaited strategy for "renewal of youth justice" will include tougher penalties for a small number of violent and repeat offenders.

The package, to be unveiled in the next few weeks, will permit the naming of some young offenders convicted of serious crimes and will allow for the transfer to adult court of more youths charged with violent offences.

Ms. McLellan has repeatedly said there are no "simplistic approaches" to the problem of youth crime, and her package will combine measures to ensure the protection of society through crime prevention and enhanced rehabilitation of young offenders.

New legislation to replace the 14-year-old Young Offenders Act will not be tabled until the fall, after another round of consultations.

The Liberals plan to introduce a significant number of changes to the existing act and believe it will be easier to craft an entirely new law than add piecemeal amendments.

But because the act has been the subject of so much criticism, they also want to signal to Canadians that an entirely new legal regime is in place. The new law would, however, preserve many of the key parts of the old act that have been seen to be working.

Ms. McLellan's plan, which has already cleared a key cabinet committee, must still be approved by the full cabinet later this week and further changes are still possible.

The package will retain a separate justice system for young offenders. Some critics have suggested the maximum age in the law be lowered from 17, but no change is contemplated.

Among the changes being considered:

- Improved sentencing options to require youths to account for their crimes, learn about the damage they caused and make reparations to the victim and community.
- More alternatives to the formal court system for youths accused of minor criminal behaviour.
- Some young offenders could be named after they are convicted of serious crimes, although in some cases judges would have the discretion to ban publication.
- A new category of offences that would require some youths to convince a judge they should remain in the youth system. Currently, 16- and 17-year-olds charged with murder, attempted murder, manslaughter and aggravated sexual assault are presumed to face trial in adult court, and the package would add young persons who demonstrate a pattern of serious, violent crimes. Some 14- and 15-year-olds would also be presumed to face adult court.

The youth reforms will come in a detailed response to last year's report by the Commons justice committee, which conducted cross-country hearings and heard from more than 300 witnesses.

The package will be the first major initiative for the justice minister from Alberta, who must attempt to reconcile Reform calls for the toughening of the law with traditional Liberal values.

In recent speeches, Ms. McLellan has said the current youth law works for about 85% of young offenders, those who are charged with property crimes and are not repeat offenders.

But she said the act's credibility has suffered because of how it is perceived to respond to violent crime.

"We must now confront the reality that the key piece of federal legislation dealing with young offenders is viewed as having little or no legitimacy," she said earlier this month. "For some, the youth justice system has sadly come to symbolize the failure of our criminal justice system to reflect the values of those it was meant to serve."

The justice minister said changes to the youth law are not the solution to the problem, and her proposals will reflect that view.

Early intervention for children at risk, prevention programs and other approaches involving families, communities, teachers and social workers are the most effective way to deal with youth crime, she has said.

"Despite what some might say, reforming our youth justice system to better reflect Canadians' concern does not mean putting kids in jail."

The preamble to the YCJA states:

AND WHEREAS Canadian society should have a youth criminal justice system that commands respect, takes into account the interests of victims, fosters responsibility and ensures accountability through meaningful consequences and effective rehabilitation and reintegration, and that reserves its most serious intervention for the most serious crimes and reduces the over-reliance on incarceration for non-violent young persons;

The preamble illustrates the core philosophy of the Act, which is essentially that not only should youth be held accountable for their actions, they should be provided with opportunities to be rehabilitated and reintegrated into society. Later, Sections 3 (1a–d) in Table 1.1 of the Act declares:

(1) The following principles apply in this Act:

    (a) the youth criminal justice system is intended to

        (i) prevent crime by addressing the circumstances underlying a young person's offending behaviour,

        (ii) rehabilitate young persons who commit offences and reintegrate them into society, and

        (iii) ensure that a young person is subject to meaningful consequences for his or her offence in order to promote the long-term protection of the public;

    (b) the criminal justice system for young persons must be separate from that of adults and emphasize the following:

        (i) rehabilitation and reintegration,

        (ii) fair and proportionate accountability that is consistent with the greater dependency of young persons and their reduced level of maturity,

        (iii) enhanced procedural protection to ensure that young persons are treated fairly and that their rights, including their right to privacy, are protected,

        (iv) timely intervention that reinforces the link between the offending behaviour and its consequences, and

(v) the promptness and speed with which persons responsible for enforcing this Act must act, given young persons' perception of time;

(c) within the limits of fair and proportionate accountability, the measures taken against young persons who commit offences should

   (i) reinforce respect for societal values,

   (ii) encourage the repair of harm done to victims and the community,

   (iii) be meaningful for the individual young person given his or her needs and level of development and, where appropriate, involve the parents, the extended family, the community and social or other agencies in the young person's rehabilitation and reintegration, and

   (iv) respect gender, ethnic, cultural and linguistic differences and respond to the needs of aboriginal young persons and of young persons with special requirements; and

(d) special considerations apply in respect of proceedings against young persons and, in particular,

   (i) young persons have rights and freedoms in their own right, such as a right to be heard in the course of and to participate in the processes, other than the decision to prosecute, that lead to decisions that affect them, and young persons have special guarantees of their rights and freedoms,

   (ii) victims should be treated with courtesy, compassion and respect for their dignity and privacy and should suffer the minimum degree of inconvenience as a result of their involvement with the youth criminal justice system,

   (iii) victims should be provided with information about the proceedings and given an opportunity to participate and be heard, and

   (iv) parents should be informed of measures or proceedings involving their children and encouraged to support them in addressing their offending behaviour.

References

Agnew R (2003) An integrated theory of the adolescent peak in offending. Youth Soc 34(3): 263–299

Albanese P (2009) Children in Canada today. Oxford University Press, Don Mills

Alvi S (1986) Realistic crime prevention strategies through alternative measures for youth. In: Currie D, MacLean BD (eds) The administration of justice, Social Research Unit, Department of Sociology, University of Saskatchewan, Saskatoon, pp 112–127

Alvi S (2007) A Criminal justice history of children and youth in Canada: taking stock in the YCJA era. In: Schissel B, Brooks C (eds) Marginality, condemnation: an introduction to criminology, 2nd edn. Fernwood, Toronto

Aries P (1962) Centuries of childhood. Vintage Books, New York

Awad GA (1987) A critique of the principles of the young offenders act. Can J Psychiatry/Revue canadienne de psychiatrie 32(6):440–443

Bala N (1997) Young offenders law. Irwin Law, Concord

Bala N, Carrington PJ, Roberts JV (2009) Evaluating the youth criminal justice act after five years: a qualified success 1. Can J Criminol Crim Justice 51(2):131–167

Barber J, Doob AN (2004) An analysis of public support for severity and proportionality in the sentencing of youthful offenders. Can J Criminol Crim Justice 46(3):327–328

Barrett M, McIntosh M (1982) The anti-social family. Verso, London

Beck U (1992) Risk society: towards a new modernity. Sage, Thousand Oaks

Bell S (2007) Young offenders and juvenile justice: a century after the fact, 3rd edn. ITP Nelson, Toronto

Canadian Bar Association (2010) National criminal justice section: Bill c-4: Youth Criminal Justice Act Amendments

Canadian Council on Social Development (2011) Average Family Income (constant 1995$). http://www.ccsd.ca/factsheets/fs_avgin.html

Caputo T, Goldenberg S (1986) Young people and the law: a consideration of luddite and utopian responses. In: MacLean BD (ed) The administration of justice, Social Research Unit, University of Saskatchewan, Saskatoon, pp 91–111

Carrigan DO (1998) Juvenile delinquency in Canada: a history. Irwin, Concord

Casavant L, Valiquet D (2010) Bill c-38: an Act to amend the royal Canadian mounted police act and to make consequential amendments to other Acts

Caston RJ (1998) Life in a business-oriented society: a sociological perspective. Allyn and Bacon, Boston

Comacchio CR (2006) The dominion of youth: adolescence and the making of a modern Canada (1920–1950). Wilfrid Laurier University Press, Waterloo

Corrado R, Markwart AE (1992) The evaluation and implementation of a new era of juvenile justice in Canada. In: Corrado R, Bala N, Linden R, Leblanc M (eds) Juvenile justice in Canada. Butterworths, Toronto, pp 35–50

Corrado RR, Markwart A (1994) The need to reform the YOA in response to violent young offenders: confusion, reality or myth. Can J Criminol 36(3):343–378

Côté JE, Allahar AL (2006) Critical youth studies: a Canadian focus. Pearson Prentice Hall, Toronto

Cullen FT, Wright JP, Chamlin MB (1999) Social support and social reform: a progressive crime control agenda. Crime Delinquency 45(2):188–207

Currie D (1986) The transformation of juvenile justice in Canada. In: MacLean BD (ed) The political economy of crime. Prentice-Hall, Toronto, pp 56–72

Currie E (2004) The road to whatever: middle-class culture and the crisis of adolescence. Henry Holt, New York

Department of Justice Canada (1999) A strategy for the renewal of youth justice

Doob AN, Cesaroni C (2004) Responding to youth crime in Canada. University of Toronto Press, Toronto

Doob A, Sprott JB (2009) Reducing child imprisonment in Canada. Crim Justice Matters 75(1):32–34

Eisler L, Schissel B (2008) Globalization, justice and the demonization of youth. Intern J Soc Inq 1(1):167–187

Foster D (2009) Locating children in the discourse of Squeegee kids. In: Lerner L (ed) Depicting Canada's children. Wilfred Laurier Press, Waterloo, pp 201–218

Gabor T (1999) Trends in youth crime: some evidence pointing to increases in the severity and volume of violence on the part of young people. Can J Criminol 41(3):385–392

Gagnon D (1984) History of the law for juvenile delinquents. Ministry of the solicitor general of Canada, government working paper no. 1984-56

Garland D (2001) The culture of control. University of Chicago Press, Chicago

Giroux HA (2009) Youth in a suspect society: democracy or disposability? Palgrave Macmillan, New York

Gleason M (2005) From "disgraceful carelessness" to "intelligent precaution": accidents and the public child in English Canada (1900–1950). J Family Hist 30(2):230–241

Hall GS (1904) Adolescence, vols 1 and 2. Appleton, New York

Hendrick H (1992) Children and childhood. Recent Find Res Econ Soc Hist 15:1–4

Heywood C (2001) A history of childhood: children and childhood in the west from medieval to modern times. Polity Press, Cambridge

Houston SE (1972) Victorian origins of juvenile delinquency: a Canadian experience. Hist Education Q 12(3):254–280

Hylton JH (1994) Get tough or get smart? Options for Canada's youth justice system in the twenty-first century. Can J Criminol 36(3):229–246

Kowalski M (1999) Alternative measures for youth in Canada (85-002-XIE/0089985-002-XIE). Canadian Centre for Justice Statistics

Leschied AW, Gendreau P (1994) Doing justice in Canada: YOA policies that can promote community safety. Can J Criminol 36(3):291–303

Matthews R (1979) Decarceration and the fiscal crisis. In: Fine B (ed) Capitalism and the rule of law. Hutchinson, London, pp 100–117

McGuire M (1997) C.19: an act to amend the young offenders act and the criminal code— "getting tougher?"(Canada). Can J Criminol 39(2):185–214

Muncie J (2006) Governing young people: coherence and contradiction in contemporary youth justice. Crit Soc Policy 26(4):770–793

Muncie J (2008) The 'punitive turn' in juvenile justice: cultures of control and rights compliance in western Europe and the USA. Youth Justice 8(2):107–121

Muncie J (2009) Youth and crime. Sage Publications, London

Neff C (2000) Youth in Canada west: a case study of Red Hill Farm School emigrants (1854–1868). J Family Hist 25(4):432–490

Neff C (2004) The education of destitute homeless children in nineteenth-century Ontario. J Family Hist 29(1):3–46

Petersen AC, Mortimer JT (1994) Youth unemployment and society. Cambridge University Press, Cambridge

Peterson-Badali M, Abramovitch R, Duda J (1997) Young children's legal knowledge and reasoning ability. Can J Criminol 39:145–170

Platt A (1977) The child savers: the invention of delinquency. University of Chicago Press, Chicago

Pulis JE, Sprott JB (2005) Probation sentences and proportionality under the young offenders act and the youth criminal justice act. Can J Criminol Crim Justice 47(4):709–723

Purkayastha B (2000) Liminal lives: South Asian youth and domestic violence. J Soc Distress Homeless 9(3):201–219

Schissel B (1993) Social dimensions of Canadian youth justice. Oxford University Press, Toronto

Sutherland N (2000) Children in English-Canadian society: framing the twentieth-century consensus. Wilfrid Laurier Press, Waterloo

Tustin L, Lutes R (2008) A guide to the Youth Criminal Justice Act–2008/09 edition. Lexis Nexis Canada Inc, Markham

Wardell B (1986) The young offenders act: a report card (1984–1986). In: Currie D (ed) The administration of justice, Social Research Unit, University of Saskatchewan, Saskatoon, pp 128–158

West WG (1984) Young offenders and the state: a Canadian perspective on delinquency. Butterworths, Toronto

Young J (1999) The exclusive society. Sage, London

Young J (2007) The Vertigo of late modernity. Sage, London

Chapter 2
Young People in Contemporary Canada

Abstract People do not exist in a vacuum. Our social environment *conditions* our behaviour by setting limits on our life chances. Put differently, not everyone is born into the same social circumstances, and this inequality of condition sets the boundaries within which people make their lives. If we are to understand the status and behaviour, "good or bad", of Canada's youth, we must take account of their social circumstances. This chapter provides an overview of some key economic and social factors affecting young people's lives.

Young people in late modern societies face a scrutiny that barely conceals a culture of abandonment and ephebiphobia, a term meaning fear or loathing of young people. In the UK and the Netherlands, paraprofessional police are hired to patrol areas where teenagers often "hang out" (Jacobson and Saville 1999; Scott and Services 2002) or videotaped by police in inconspicuous vehicles. In Cincinnati, youth are escorted around malls (see Box 2.1). Also in the United States, Giroux reports that (2009, p. 73) in the state of Washington, fourth grade reading scores and graduation rates are used as a planning tool to determine how many prison cells should be built, a rationality that affirms the well-known link between educational performance and delinquency, but also underscores a banal acceptance of the idea that there is nothing we can do to help children improve school performance, so we might as well plan for failure. In Quebec, convenience stores tested high pitched irritating sound emitters that only people under 25 can hear as a "solution" to the perceived problem of unruly teens (White et al. 2011).

Has Canada created a culture in which control, surveillance, and criminalization of youth trump intelligently designed evidence-based policies focusing on the real causes of youth transgression? In this chapter, I want to provide an analysis of the notion of the risky child. What constitutes such risk? Who are the children who are most at risk, and why? To provide answers to these questions, this chapter examines the status of Canadian children in a number of domains, economic, education, and health, and relates this status to a number of important trends in Canada. It documents the ways in which children and childhood and youth are

S. Alvi, *Youth Criminal Justice Policy in Canada*, SpringerBriefs in Criminology, DOI: 10.1007/978-1-4419-0273-3_2, © The Author(s) 2012

conditioned by social relations, at the macro level, focusing particularly on the late modern era (1950s on), and the implications of that conditioning. It also pays attention to the kinds of social support available to children and families, and how this social support in turn was conditioned by macro level social relations. I will turn first to a discussion of the macro level economic characteristics of late modern societies.

Box 2.1 Mall Implements 'Youth Escort Policy'

Posted: 08/06/2010
By: Adam Marshall
CINCINNATI - As you walk through the doors at Tri-County Mall on a Friday or Saturday night you'll now see security guards checking identification for everyone who looks under 25.
It's all part of the new Youth Escort Policy.
The new rules require anyone under the age of 18 to have an escort with them 21 years of age or older.
The policy applies every Friday and Saturday from 4 p.m. to close.
Management at Tri-County Mall says it should make for a more pleasant shopping experience for their customers.
"Being youth, and being in large numbers unsupervised, they tend to get loud and rowdy and detract from a comfortable shopping atmosphere.," said General Manager Michael Lyons.
To enforce the rules, there will be extra security at every entrance of the mall.
Some customers say the new rules are not necessary, while others agree with what mall management is trying to do.
"To this extent? Wristbands and security at every door, it's not fair. It's not right," said 18 year-old Jahnise Bowie.
"Doing nothing but hanging out that that can be disruptive and therefore I'm OK with that part of it. But on the other hand, if you have a teenager that is here to shop, and that person is here to just pick up an item or two, I think he or she should be able to do that as well," said customer Derwin Jamison.
Management says they understand not everyone will be thrilled with the new policy, however the long-term effect on mall business should be positive.
"I think it's important to remember that this program is only going to be in place Friday evenings and Saturday evenings. There are five other days when the program isn't going to be in place at all," Lyons said.
Other facilities in the area do have similar policies, however none are this strict.
Copyright (c) 2010 The E. W. Scripps Company

Capitalism, Late Modernity and Youth

A number of scholars have recently been preoccupied with explaining the contours and consequences of social problems within the context of late modernity. Writers such as Young (2007b), Bauman (2000; 2005) and Beck (1992) have argued that the conditions of life in the present period are fundamentally different from those that existed in the Post World War II era, mainly in terms of the centrality of social exclusion as a mode of organizing people, and within the context of the rise of neo-liberalism, a term that I define following Giroux (2004, p. 13) who characterizes it as a "virulent and brutal form of market capitalism…[in which] everything is for sale or plundered for profit." David Harvey (Harvey 2010, p. 10) argues further that the term refers to:

> …a class project that coalesced in the crisis of the 1970s. Masked by a lot of rhetoric about individual freedom, liberty, personal responsibility, and the virtues of privatization, the free market and free trade, it legitimized draconian policies designed to restore and consolidate capitalist class power. This project has been successful, judging by the incredible centralization of wealth and power observable in all those countries that took the neoliberal road. And there is no evidence that it is dead.

Thus, for these and other commentators, the current period of *late modernity*— the term I will use to characterize the era throughout this book—is one in which the rise of individualism, and the concomitant phenomenon of responsibilization are rooted in a globalized neo-liberal ethos existing side by side with neo-con-servative political and economic strategies, including managerialism and risk management (Muncie 2006). Building on the work of Eric Hobsbawm and Stan Cohen, Young (2007a) maintains that in contrast to the two decades of prosperity and relative stability following the Second World War, the late 1960s witnessed an unraveling of these stable relations, fueled by a cultural revolution and funda-mental economic restructuring which essentially transformed societies and global relations. In the midst of these transformations, youth came to be seen as the harbingers of new cultural forms that were in many respects seen as alien and disagreeable by the adults around them. Indeed, youth themselves were active agents in this process, a point, Young reminds us, often ignored in the moral panic literature, but critical to understanding youth acts of deviance as intentional and "fun" (Katz 1988). In this dialectic of the moral panic over youth (captured by the oft-heard term, "what is wrong with young people today?") and young people's active resistance and even enjoyment of the world they were creating, adults felt that the stable, disciplined, and predictable world as they had known it was slip-ping away (Young 2007a).

More recently, a new kind of moral panic and othering has occurred in a set of new contexts. The steady decline in manufacturing industries in Western societies and the corresponding rise of menial, dead-end jobs in the service sector (most of which offer minimal or no benefits, low wages, and no job security), has created a culture of resentment and a "generalized feeling of unfairness, a failure of meri-tocracy which is underscored by widespread redundancies and changes in career"

(Young 2007b, p. 4). The response to this, he argues, is two variants of othering. Conservative othering "projects negative attributes on the other and thereby grants positive attributes to oneself" (Young 2007b, p. 5). Liberal othering, on the other hand, is less likely to be acknowledged, and occurs when "the other is seen to lack our qualities and virtues...as a deficit which is caused by a deprivation of material or cultural circumstances or capital. They would be *just like us* if these circumstances improved" (Young 2007b, p. 5). In effect, today adults are not scared of the loss of discipline and predictability in the face of cultural transformation experienced in the 1960s, we are instead worried about the loss of jobs and income security, a middle class "vertigo" or "fear of falling" from the hitherto contended, but increasingly precarious ranks of the middle classes (Ehrenreich 1990).

These transformations are fundamentally different from other historical periods because the political economic conditions that now prevail in Western societies, including Canada, are fundamentally different than they were during the post-war period. To illustrate, let us turn to David Harvey's analysis of the political economy of the current age. Harvey (Harvey 2010, pp. 40–46) reminds us that capital is a process by which money goes in search of more money. There are many ways that this process can be realized, including finance markets, production of goods and services, and rent on property. The dominant form of capital circulation for a very long time has involved the production of goods, in which the capitalist provides capital input to purchase materials, labour, and the tools of production, which then are deployed to create goods, which in turn are sold in the market for a profit. A fraction of those profits are then reinvested in the process as fresh capital so that the process can begin again. Two central principles driving the success of this process are the speed and spatial circulation of capital. In other words, the faster a factory can make goods without sacrificing quality, using new technologies in particular, the more likely they are to accrue higher profits at the expense of their competitors. At the same time, if money is invested in technologies or labour that exist in a location that must be used in a different place, it is imperative that those technologies or labour power can be deployed with a minimal amount of delay due to geographical constraints. Similarly, geographical barriers to trade can greatly impede the realization of profits.

Harvey goes on to argue that historically, and notwithstanding the role of counteracting tendencies such as protectionism, war or other crises, there has been a general trend towards the elimination of spatial barriers and an increase in the velocity of money. One consequence of these trends is an increase in surplus capital seeking reinvestment to fuel continued growth. If such growth is blocked, then capital over-accumulates and becomes devalued, taking the concrete form of closed factories, abandoned businesses, and a surfeit of commodities that cannot be sold. In turn, rates of return on investment are reduced or eliminated altogether, and the value of stocks, shares, and property declines.

What are the social correlates of this process? While capitalism has proven to be remarkably resilient over the past 200 years, this resilience has not come without costs, sometimes violent ones. One associated consequence has been the concentration of wealth in the hands of a minority at the expense of the vast majority of working and middle class people. Indeed, the paradox of capitalism has been that it has created astonishing wealth to the tune of $2.4 trillion dollars in the hands of 793 billionaires as of 2009 (of whom 20 were Canadian), and shameful poverty in the hands of the 40% of the working poor in the world who work for less than $2 a day (Therborn 2011, p. 190). Another has been state intervention to sustain failing businesses via bailouts as most recently occurred in the 2008 crisis. Wars are fought to secure new markets, geopolitical advantage, or sources of raw materials. And, when capital sits idle, it becomes important to find new ways to encourage consumers to buy, which in turn is the major motivation for the rise of the massive credit industry, and the trillions of dollars spent on advertising every year. Thus, capitalism has reached a point in history where capitalist states (which are far more than governments) are now irrevocably yoked to business ideology and goals. And these goals increasingly trump the needs of families, youth, and children through a dual process in which fewer financial and social resources are made available for those in need via the dismantling of the welfare state, while at the same time those same people are told that they are responsible for their own well-being. Thus, we are witnessing an individualization of social problems coupled with demonization of those who are most at risk of experiencing the consequences of those problems. In the meantime, running apace, is a culture of fear of the dangerous "other," who are very often youth, cheerfully replicated and amplified by the popular media.

But what does this short analysis of the logics of the capitalist mode of production and the ideology that accompanies it have to do with justice for children and youth? There are many ways to connect these processes with the lives of young people, and I first want to address the issue of income and wealth disparity.

The Economic Status of Youth and Their Families

Children are poor because their families are poor. When families are economically disadvantaged, their children face reduced opportunities to participate in legitimate everyday life. Moreover, there is now incontrovertible evidence that children who receive proper care, nurturance, food, and social support enjoy far greater advantages as they move through the life-course. Economic instability, glossed over by the media and the state by the ideology of the "new" economy and the "inevitability" of hard choices has created immense hardship for many Canadian families. Economic instability not only creates under- and unemployment it has also forced many people to work at two or more jobs, and to work harder and faster, for less pay, and diminished or non-existent benefits. According to the Canadian Index of Wellbeing Network (Arundel 2009, p. 5):

> ...22 percent of all Canadian workers earned two-thirds or less of the median earnings for Canadians. And the proportion of low wage workers is growing: between 2000 and 2008, the proportion of minimum wage jobs grew from 4.7 percent to 5.2 percent of all jobs and the number working at minimum wage grew by three quarters of a million workers. While

many of these jobs may be held by young people starting out, four in ten of them in 2007 were held by people over the age of 25 years.

Thus, while some people are economically speaking, "treading water", many others end up falling through the cracks of the economic system, creating higher rates of family stress, poverty, disenfranchisement, resentment, and bitterness.

The most recent recession, which some commentators are calling the worst since the Great Depression of the 1930s, was due mostly to rash lending practices in the sub-prime mortgage sector of the US economy which forced some lending institutions into bankruptcy and necessitated bailouts to others from the US government. Consequently, stock markets worldwide crashed, creating a global recession (Arsenault and Sharpe 2009). Despite historical evidence that tax cuts to businesses do not promote investment (Stanford 2011), the Canadian federal government continues to insist otherwise, taking refuge in tried neo-liberal economic policies, while broadcasting Canada's resilience in the face of the recession (See Box 2.2). Yet, data on the well-being of vulnerable groups, including youth, indicate that many aspects of these people's lives have gotten worse over the years prior to the recession, and in many domains of well-being their problems have amplified post recession.

Box 2.2. Update: Canada's Flaherty: Economy Remains Government's Top Priority

January 13, 2011
By Karen Johnson Of DOW JONES NEWSWIRES
VAUGHAN, Ont. (Dow Jones)—Canada's Economic Action Plan continues to create jobs and stimulate growth, Canadian Finance Minister Jim Flaherty said Monday.

"The economy remains our government's number one priority, and with the global economy still fragile, we continue to focus on creating jobs and economic growth," Flaherty said, speaking at the Earth Rangers nature and education center outside of Toronto.

Flaherty was delivering the seventh report on the Economic Action Plan—a $60 billion boost to the Canadian economy announced in 2009. He said the action plan shielded Canadians from "the worst of the financial crisis" and "is now positioning Canada to succeed in what is a highly competitive economy."

He said the Conservative government remains "committed to keeping taxes low for job creators." He said in its previous two budgets, the Conservative government has announced the elimination of all remaining tariffs on machinery and equipment and manufacturing inputs. He called it a "permanent benefit that sets our nation apart for all the right reasons," Flaherty said.

"Canada will be the first tariff-free zone for industrial manufacturers in the entire G20," Flaherty said.

Flaherty also said reducing the corporate tax rate helps stimulate job growth and investment. The federal rate was lowered this year to 16.5%, from 18% last year. It's slated to drop to 15% next year.

The main opposition Liberal party has called for the tax cut to be rolled back, saying it's not affordable as Canada seeks to balance its budget over the medium term.

The 2011 budget, which Flaherty said will be released sometime in March, is expected to be controversial and could trigger an election. It would be the third election in five years.

Canada is on track to return to balanced budgets ahead of its G7 peers, job creation is close to 400,000 jobs—nearly 85% of them full-time—virtually offsetting all of the jobs lost during the recession.

"Two years after introducing the Economic Action Plan, Canada has come out of the global darkness in the strongest position in the [Group of Seven leading nations]," Flaherty said.

He said there are two major threats to the Canadian economy: weakness in U.S. consumer spending and the instability in some euro-zone nations.

"Without question, global economic stability is far from assured," he said. Citing "candid conversations" with other world leaders at the World Economic Forum over the weekend in Davos, Switzerland, Flaherty said "the world is not lacking in challenges."

"Other nations continue to grapple with potentially unsustainable public debt loads and lingering concerns about their financial systems," he said.

Such instability globally makes Canada's performance "all the more remarkable," he said.

- By Karen Johnson, Dow Jones Newswires; 416-306-2022; karen.johnson@dowjones.com

In addition to high unemployment and under-employment, other indicators point to a system that is failing youth and children. While the incidence of child poverty has dropped since the 1990s, approximately 1 in 10 children still live below the poverty line (see Table 2.1) despite a House of Commons resolution in 1989 to eliminate child poverty by the year 2000. About one-third of these children belong to families where a parent is working full time (Campaign 2000, 2010). Not surprisingly, child poverty rates have historically increased during, and in the aftermath of, recessions (Yalnizyan, 2010). The problem is far worse for Aboriginal children. In cities of more than 100,000, half of the Aboriginal children under 15 live in low-income housing compared to one in five for non-Aboriginal children (Unicef 2009).

The negative impact of poverty on children has been well documented and include lower educational attainment, poor health, cognitive, and behavioural

Table 2.1 Incidence of child poverty by province, Canada, 1990–2004

Province	Year											
	1990	1991	1992	1993	1994	1995	1996	2000	2001	2002	2003	2004
Newfoundland	20.8	20.6	26.8	21.8	23.4	26.2	20.2	17.7	13.7	14.0	15.8	12.8
PEI	14.0	15.6	12.7	11.4	13.3	14.2	18.5	7.7	5.8	7.1	4.7	4.6
Nova Scotia	16.8	20.6	19.4	23.4	20.5	21.5	23.5	12.5	13.3	12.7	14.4	11.9
New Brunswick	18.6	19.2	15.9	18.0	18.3	24.4	19.8	10.5	9.5	10.3	10.9	8.8
Québec	19.5	20.4	19.3	21.4	19.8	22.6	22.0	16.0	14.5	11.3	10.9	10.9
Ontario	14.8	17.3	16.3	20.8	18.1	19.1	20.3	12.8	10.3	11.7	11.4	12.8
Manitoba	24	30.9	24.2	26.1	22.8	23.2	26.6	16.7	15.6	16.2	16.9	12.8
Saskatchewan	21.8	22.4	24.0	24.8	22.9	21.8	22.3	13.0	10.7	8.9	12.9	10.9
Alberta	19.8	19.2	24.5	20.6	18.5	21.7	20.7	12.3	10.9	9.2	11.0	11.7
British Columbia	17.6	14.4	19.3	21.5	21.2	20.8	20.2	14.1	14.0	18.3	18.7	18.1
Canada	17.8	18.9	19.2	21.3	19.5	21.0	21.1	13.8	12.1	12.2	12.5	12.8

Source Prepared by the Centre for International Statistics at the Canadian Council on Social Development, using data from Statistics Canada, Cat. 13-569-XPB for years 1990 to 1996, and Statistics Canada. Income Trends in Canada 2004, Cat. 75-202-XIE for years 2000 to 2004
Note Children under 18 years of age. Based on Statistics Canada's Low-income Cut-offs, 1992 base

problems that will often shape and determine a young person's life course (Willms, 2002), including delinquent and criminal behaviour (Jarjoura, Triplett and Brinker, 2002)

If children's parents are having difficulty finding and keeping meaningful, well-paying work, the same can be said for young people of working age. Between 1984 and 1994 the real median income of young people fell by 23%, and the unemployment rate among youth aged 15 to 24 has consistently been double the rates for adults (Rehnby and McBride 1997). Between 1989 and 1999, following a recession at the beginning of the decade, the proportion of 16-year-olds who had never had a job increased from 26 to 58% (Canadian Council on Social Development, 1999). At the same time, the average young person in Canada earned less in 1997 than they were earning in the 1980s, reflecting a shift in the nature of work towards low-paying, part-time jobs as food servers and store clerks (Canadian Council on Social Development, 1999). Further, the participation of young people in the labour market dropped by over 10 % in the 1990s alone, and the gap between the youth and overall employment rates continues to grow. Overall, unemployment rates for young people attending school, as illustrated in Fig. 2.1 have remained high in Canada for the past three decades.

In past economic downturns, many Canadians were able to cope with unemployment because of the Unemployment Insurance scheme that had been in place. But as Yalnizyan (2009, p. 5) remarks, by the 1990s, the policy (now renamed Employment Insurance) had been "gutted," such that:

In the last recession, 85% of unemployed men and 81% of unemployed women could rely on benefits if they lost their job; today only 45% of men and 39% of women can. The last time the unemployed were this exposed to economic risk was in the 1940s.

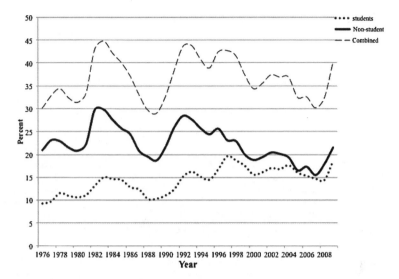

Fig. 2.1 Canada unemployment rate: Labour force survey estimates (LFS), by full- and part-time students age 15–19, during school months, unadjusted for seasonality, computed annual average, 1976–2009 *Source* Derived from: Statistics Canada. *Table 282-0005-Labour force survey estimates (LFS), by full- and part-time students during school months, sex and age group, unadjusted for seasonality, computed annual average (persons unless otherwise noted)*, CANSIM (database), Using E-STAT (distributor)http://estat.statcan.gc.ca.uproxy.library.dc-uoit.ca/cgi-win/cnsmcgi.exe?Lang=E&EST-Fi=EStat/English/CII_1-eng.htm

The unemployment problem is even more acute for recent (within the past five years) immigrants to Canada. Among those immigrants with university degrees, the rate of unemployment was more than four times that of non-immigrants with degrees in 2009 (2010). An aging population, declining fertility rates, and overall smaller families has driven aggressive immigration policies such that Canada now accepts nearly a quarter of a million newcomers per year. Thus, the Community Foundations of Canada group states that immigration will become the sole source of population growth by 2030 (2010, pp. 2–3). Because of the way that Canada's immigration laws are structured, many people admitted to the country are highly educated and skilled, yet they face numerous obstacles to participation in work life, including language barriers, lack of work experience, and non-recognition of professional designations or qualifications. Indeed, only about one quarter of these workers are working in the fields they were trained in, compared to nearly two-thirds of Canadian born workers (2010, p. 3).

Late modern economies require technical skills and expertise, yet young people are being forced into a "prolonged state of social marginality" (Petersen and Mortimer 1994). In effect, although employment during adolescence could provide significant experiences for growth into later work roles, as well as a sense of belonging to the conventional social order, for some time now Canadian society has been unable to provide many youth with such meaningful work experiences.

Ironically, though youth unemployment is high, our society places tremendous pressures on youth to consume goods and services that they may not be able to afford. In 2005, Canadian youth spent $2.9 billion of their own money, more than double of what they spent in 1995, and influenced the purchasing habits of their parents to the tune of more than $20 billion (Canadian Teachers Federation, 2006). As Caston(1998)points out, along with the family and schools, advertising is one of the most important agents of socialization in our society, and thus fosters:

> ...a market orientation by depicting consumption as an end in itself and as a measure of social status and human value. Whether it is hawking overpriced designer jeans and underwear, prescription drugs, credit cards, or any one of tens of thousands of other products and services, advertising's messages to us are "be a consumer," "spend it now," "live for today," "your worth is measured by the name brands you buy." (1998, p. 248)

At the same time that young people are told that they have "multiple choice freedoms," (Côté and Allahar 2006, p. 78) then, they are also being told that such freedom belongs in the realm of choice over the numerous empty status symbols constituting youth markets. And as Cote and Allahar argue, they are also told that they are responsible for their own choices and destinies, but as the arguments that follow will show, many do not have access to the kinds of legitimate opportunities that foster success.

Families also look very different than they did four decades ago. The main family form between the early 1900s and the 1950s was what is sometimes called the "traditional nuclear" family, consisting of a mother at home, a working father, and usually two or more children. In 1981 the majority (84%) of children lived with married parents, but this dropped to just over two-thirds by 2001 (See Table 2.2). As of 2000, almost 279,000 children under the age of 12 lived in blended families, and another 733,000 under age 15 lived with common law parents, more than four times the proportion in 1981. In addition, birth rates have remained low in Canada for decades, and families have become smaller than they were in the 1950s and 1960s (Canadian Council on Social Development, 2006).

In addition, the majority (85%) of two-parent families are dual income couples, and two-thirds of women with young children under the age of 6 are employed. Yet most have very little economic security because real incomes (income in constant dollars) have remained relatively stable since the 1990s (See Table 2.3) and female lone parents consistently earn less than their male or two parent counterparts. In other words, many families are working twice as hard to maintain the standard of living they would have enjoyed nearly 20 years ago. This pressure is compounded by the enormous debt load being carried by most Canadian families, who between 1984 and 2009 more than doubled their household debt. Again, lone parent families suffered the highest debt-to-income ratios (Hurst 2011).

Other factors have contributed to changes in the nature of families. Divorce rates rose dramatically in Canada when the country liberalized its divorce laws in the 1960s. This is not to say, of course, that divorced parents are any less likely to provide a loving, nurturing environment in which children can grow up. However, divorce does have some important implications for family life. For instance,

Table 2.2 Distribution of children aged 0–11 by family type, 1981 and 2001

Family type	1981	1991	2001
Living with married parents	84	77	68
Living with common-law parents	3	7	13
Living with a lone parent	13	18	19

Source Adapted from (Jenson 2003, p. 40)

research in both Canada and the United States has consistently shown that women fare far worse economically than men after divorce, and that in fact, the economic status of males after divorce actually improves (Finnie 1993; Smock 1993, 1994). Thus, the experience of divorce is economically gendered. Another consequence of the unequal experience of divorce is that many single-parent female headed families experience high rates of poverty (Casper et al. 1994). In fact, in 2008, the child poverty rate was 38% for female-led single parent families, while about half of female lone mothers with children under the age of six live in poverty (Campaign 2000, 2010).

Thus, according to Eshlemen (1997, p. 241):
Single parent families are characterized by a high rate of poverty, a high percentage age of minority representation, more dependents, relatively low education, and a high rate of mobility...psychologically, single parents are more depressed, are more anxious, have poorer self images, and are less satisfied with their lives.

Recent data from an ongoing national survey of young people in Canada indicate that many children from single mother, poor families suffer a range of problems, many of which are linked to deviant behaviour (See Table 2.4). The important point here is that while such problems occur in high and low income families, it is the most disadvantaged families that seem to experience them the most. This does not mean however, that criminal or deviant behaviour is a property of the "lower classes," but it does mean that children living in such circumstances face higher risks for criminal behaviour.

It might seem obvious that children are adversely affected by divorce. However, there is some controversy over this view. It is true that divorce has negative economic and social consequences for children. For instance, as Eshleman (1997) points out, adolescents from divorced homes are less likely to graduate from high school, have a lower probability of ever marrying, and greater chances of getting divorced themselves. In addition, there is some evidence to suggest that children from such homes are more likely to commit crime, and experience problems in relating to peers (Juby and Farrington 2001; Wells and Ranken 1991).

What is uncertain is the extent to which such problems actually come from the *relationships* between family members *during* the marriage. It may be, then, that parental conflict, abuse, or persistent economic stress may actually be the factors that influence children in negative ways, and not the actual strain of divorce and separation itself. Indeed, the Caledon Institute (Jamieson and Hart, 2003, p. 3) reminds us that:

Table 2.3 Average income after tax by family type 1989–2008

Year	Two parent families with children	Male lone-parent families	Female lone-parent families
Constant 2008 $			
1989	66,900	53,600	31,900
1990	65,100	44,500	28,900
1991	63,000	42,000	28,100
1992	64,100	42,800	29,100
1993	61,800	39,200	28,600
1994	62,900	39,300	29,900
1995	62,700	39,200	29,800
1996	63,000	41,500	27,800
1997	64,100	40,900	28,500
1998	68,000	44,500	30,000
1999	70,200	44,600	31,300
2000	72,800	48,100	33,600
2001	75,500	46,800	35,400
2002	76,200	47,500	33,000
2003	76,800	50,500	33,200
2004	79,600	48,100	34,000
2005	77,900	54,900	38,400
2006	79,900	57,000	38,700
2007	83,900	53,300	40,400
2008	84,900	54,200	41,300

Source Adapted from Statistics Canada, CANSIM, table 202-0603 and Catalogue no. 75-202-X

...crime stems from a variety of critical experiences in people's lives: family violence; poor parenting; negative school experiences; poor housing; a lack of recreational, health and environmental facilities; inadequate social support; peer pressure; unemployment; and lack of opportunity and poverty. [A social development approach to dealing with crime]...emphasizes investing in individuals, families and communities by providing social, recreational, educational and economic interventions and support programs for those Canadians, mainly young people, who are most at risk of becoming involved in crime, before they come into conflict with the law.

Regardless of the implications of such debates, it is clear that many Canadian youth are today more likely to grow up in single-parent female headed homes than their predecessors a generation ago. These family circumstances place them at some risk of experiencing poverty and a host of other social pathologies, including criminality. It should be noted that the absence of a male parent is not the reason these children are more at risk. Rather, they are at risk because single-parent mothers are far more likely to be poor or working for low wages. To be sure, there are also young people in Canada who do not experience such deprivation, and whose paths to higher social and economic status seem less littered with obstacles. As we shall see, however, although criminal behaviour cuts across income levels, poor youth are significantly more "at risk" of encountering the criminal justice process (Bartollas 1997).

Table 2.4 Rates of problems for children from single-mother families compared with those of children from two-parent families, by income

Type of problem	Rates of problems by income (%)			
	Low income		Not low income	
	Single mother	Two parent	Single mother	Two parent
Hyperactivity	16.7	9.6	13.7	9.6
Conduct Disorder	19.2	9.2	13.2	7.9
Emotional Disorder	16.7	8.6	11.6	7.3
One or more behaviour problems	33.5	21.0	27.9	18.3
Repeated a grade	12.5	7.9	9.1	4.1
Social impairment	7.4	4.6	3.8	2.1
One or more total problems[a]	43.5	28.9	35.8	22.6

Source Adapted from Canada, National Longitudinal Survey of Children and Youth, 1996: 88
[a] Data available for 6–11-year-old children only. All other variables use data from 4- to 11-year-old children

Moreover, the recent crisis of capitalism will undoubtedly result in higher rates of poverty and misery for many Canadian children and their families, and, as Arsenault and Sharpe (2009, p. 29) maintain, "it will be many years before we return to the unemployment and poverty levels enjoyed before the recession hit."

Education

As numerous studies have pointed out, the young person's experience of school is an important factor in understanding youth crime (Lochner and Moretti 2001). According to the Canadian Centre for Justice Statistics (Canadian Centre for Justice Statistics, 1998), "lack of attachment to school is a significant risk factor in youth crime," primarily because such individuals are more likely to experience under- or unemployment, and are more likely to become involved with high risk behaviours such as regular alcohol or drug use. About one in five (18%) of youth between 18 and 20 left school without graduating in 1991 for a variety of reasons including, boredom, the perception that school rules are too stringent, associating with peers who attach little value to education, and for many teenage girls, pregnancy (Canadian Council on Social Development, 1998, p. 58). Today, about 7 million people of working age in Canada do not possess the literacy skills required to participate in the workforce, and nearly a third of young people read at a level 3 reading proficiency (on a scale of 5) (Arundel et al. 2009).

However, most Canadian children go to school, do reasonably well there, and go on to attend institutions of higher education. In 1994, there were 5.5 million students in elementary and high schools—almost 100% enrolment. Canada also has one of the highest enrolments in post-secondary institutions among industrialized countries. In 1994, there were 1.5 million students, or 53% of youth aged 18 to 24, enrolled in colleges, technical institutes, or universities on a part-time or full-time basis, and by 2001, almost three quarters of young people between the ages of 20 and 22 had participated in post secondary education (Lambert et al. 2004). Still, the education system is changing. Consider the following facts:

- Recent provincial cutbacks mean that many parents of elementary and secondary school students must now pay user fees for activities that were previously free, including cultural and sporting activities and special services such as speech therapy. Compulsory fees in Canadian universities have risen by 7% in 2010/11 compared to one year earlier. In 2002, two parent families spent an average of $1,464 on education-related expenses, an increase of 23% from 1999 (Canadian Council on Social Development, 2006, p. 18)
- At the post-secondary level, tuition fees are rising; Nearly half of post-secondary students require government loans to finance their education. In 2005, 44% of all graduates from college and university were in debt to government student loan programs and owed an average of $16,500 (Canada).
- Despite some progress in funding for kindergarten programs across Canada, we lag far behind most European countries where universal educational programs are provided for children aged three to five (Ontario 2008).
- A study of 9-year olds in the National Longitudinal survey of Youth found that those living in low income households tended to have lower achievement than children from more affluent households on many measures (Thomas 2009).

These data illustrate the changing nature of the Canadian educational system. They are important because of the positive association between education and the type of job one can expect to hold in adulthood. In addition, however, it is clear that poorer children are the ones who will be most affected by some of the recent shifts described above. For instance, we know that poverty negatively affects family functioning and children's school results. Data from the 1994 National Longitudinal Survey of Children and Youth "indicates that rates of family dysfunction and parental depression are higher in poor families than in more affluent families, and that poor children do not have the same scholastic and verbal skills entering school as their non-poor peers" (Canadian Council on Social Development 1997, p. 1).

Health

As with income inequality, there is increasing health disparity in Canada (Unicef 2009), and the two issues are related. The most recent report on the health of school-age children in Canada notes that despite some reductions from 2002 in consumption of sweets, daily smoking, drinking alcohol, trying cannabis, and sexual harassment, there are still some troubling issues (Boyce et al. 2007, pp 9):

- Almost half of Grade 6–10 young people in Canada are physically inactive, with the problem being particularly worrisome in girls and older students.

- Fewer than half of students indicate that they consume fruits or vegetables at least once a day.
- Approximately 26% of boys and 17% of girls are either overweight or obese.
- Obesity among young people shows an increase from 4% in 2002 to 6% in 2006.
- Just under one-third of Canadian Grade 9 and 10 students indicate that they have smoked a cigarette.
- Over half of Grade 9 and 10 students report having tried alcohol by the time they were 15 years old.
- 22% of students in Grades 9 and 10 report having had sexual intercourse.
- Just under two-fifths of students report being victims of bullying.
- Reports of racial bullying show a slight increase from 2002 to 2006.
- 14% of boys who carry weapons report that they carry handguns or other fire-arms. More girls than boys who carry weapons report carrying tear gas or pepper spray.
- About 1 in 5 students typically miss one or more days of school or other usual activities in a 12-month period due to an injury.
- The percentage of injuries that happen during organized activities tends to increase with advancing grade.
- By Grade 10, girls clearly are experiencing poorer emotional health than boys.

Not surprisingly, these issues are connected in complicated ways to the social contexts in which youth live, including their family, educational, and socio-economic settings. For instance, recent research has called for a better under-standing of the social and cultural correlates of suicide (Canada 2003), which is the second leading cause of death among 15–24 year olds in Canada, (with accidents and homicide being first and third respectively). Among Aboriginal youth, who face some of the most difficult social and economic problems, the suicide rate is five to six times higher compared to their non-Aboriginal counterparts (Canada 2002).

Corporal punishment of children by parents in Canada is still prevalent, despite the fact that numerous studies have shown that spanking does not reduce deviant behaviour, and in fact increases psychological stress and the probability of anti-social behaviour (Straus et al. 1997; Taylor et al. 2010; Turner 2002). Moreover, a study of changes in anti-social behaviour before and after Sweden banned corporal punishment in 1979 suggests that youth have demonstrated "substantial improve-ment" in well-being in the years after the ban, and although causality was not inferred, it would seem that corporal punishment is not necessary to improve the well-being of young people in that country (Durrant 2000). In spite of these findings, and the fact that many countries in Europe have followed Sweden's lead and have now banned corporal punishment, most Canadian parents see nothing wrong in disciplining their children by hitting them, and Canadian law on the matter tends to emphasize parental rights to hit rather than children's rights not to be.

Thus, in the context of increasing acceptance within medicine and the helping professions that the determinants of health and well-being are social, it is crucial that social and economic supports be buttressed and made more robust. But this is not happening. As Eisler and Schissel (Eisler and Schissel 2008, pp. 168–169) write, in the late 1970s Established Program Financing trimmed federal transfer payments while decreasing equalization payments to the provinces:

> This trend continued with the election of a majority Liberal government whose 1995 budget sought to reduce the deficit by 13.6 billion dollars over two years through a combination of spending cuts and modest tax increases. Social security transfers to the provinces were targeted as the primary recipient of governmental cutbacks (Johnson 1997). The federal government reduced monetary transfers to the provinces by 2.5 billion dollars in 1996-97 and 4.5 billion in 1997-98. This followed an initial cut of 1.5 billion dollars in transfer payments in 1994 and a decrease of 5 billion dollars to the Canadian Assistance Plan and post-secondary education and health in 1994-95. As well, a new block fund, the Canadian Health and Social Transfer program, was created through the amalgamation of the Canadian Assistance Program and funding for health and post-secondary education.

Again, this trend towards devolution of federal and eventually provincial responsibility for financing social programs has its roots in a neo-liberal agenda underscored by the assumption that markets should dictate social well-being, and that the coupling of free-market ideology with the welfare of children and families is both inevitable and desirable. Further, the ideology of "trickle down" responsibilization locates the causes of social problems such as health inequity, economic inequality, and crime in the alleged deficits of individuals, their peers, families and communities, rather than focusing analysis on social and economic conditions (Bottrell 2009). The transition to well paying, meaningful employment which is predicated on education, healthy living and above all, the availability of jobs is more precarious now than it has ever been. And this precarious world, as Jock Young (2007b, p. 12) characterizes it fosters "a sense of insecurity of insubstantiality, and of uncertainty, a whiff of chaos and a fear of falling." And it is in this context that we witness:

> The obsession with rules, an insistence on clear uncompromising lines of demarcation between correct and incorrect behaviour, a narrowing of borders, the decreased tolerance of deviance, a disproportionate response to rule-breaking, an easy resort to punitiveness and a point at which simple punishment begins to verge on the vindictive.

Instead of after-school programs, then, we have surveillance. Rather than employment training, we have growing under-and unemployment and a rise in the proportion of children under 18 using food banks from 38% in 1989 to 42% by 2004 (Canadian Council on Social Development 2006). And as a cure for the putative problem of unruly youth we have high pitched sound emitters instead of clean, safe places where youth can hang out. As the late Ian Taylor (1999) reminds us, capitalist societies have never been very supportive of the young. Nor have they been particularly kind to them in the media, which continues to play on unsubstantiated public fears about disorderly youth thereby amplifying both the magnitude and character of youth crime.

Thus, it should be clear from the arguments and data in this chapter that children and youth do not exist in a vacuum. Our social environment conditions our behaviour by setting limits on our life chances. Put differently, not everyone is born into the same social circumstances, and this inequality of condition sets the boundaries within which people make their lives. If we are to understand the status and behaviour, "good or bad", of Canada's youth, we must take account of their social circumstances. This chapter has provided a necessarily brief overview of some of the key social and economic factors facing Canadian youth with the aim of giving the reader a basic understanding of the role of market economies and the social upheaval they tend to generate. An understanding of context, is essential to understanding the nexus of crime and youth. In the following chapter, I present data on the nature and contours of youth crime in Canada.

References

Arundel C et al (2009) How are Canadians really doing? a closer look at select groups. Canadian Index of Wellbeing

Arsenault JF, Sharpe A (2009) The economic crisis through the lens of economic wellbeing. Institute of Wellbeing

Bartollas C (1997) Juvenile delinquency. Allyn and Bacon, Boston

Bauman Z (2000) Liquid modernity. Polity Press, Cambridge

Bauman Z (2005) Liquid life. Polity Press, Cambridge

Beck U (1992) Risk society: towards a new modernity. Sage, Thousand Oaks

Bottrell D (2009) Dealing with disadvantage: resilience and the social capital of young people's networks. Youth Soc 40(4):476–501

Boyce WF, King MA, Roche J (2007) Healthy settings for young people in Canada. Health Canada, Ottawa

Campaign 2000 (2010) 2010 report card on child and family poverty in Canada: 1989–2010. Campaign 2000

Canadian Centre for Justice Statistics (1998) A profile of youth justice in Canada. Statistics Canada

Canadian Council on Social Development (1997) The progress of Canada's children. Canadian Council on Social Development

Canadian Council on Social Development (1999) Youth at work in Canada: a research report. Canadian Council on Social Development

Canadian Council on Social Development (2006) The progress of Canada's children and youth 2006. Canadian Council on Social Development, Canada

Canada S Profile of debt to government student loan programs for graduates owing at graduation. http://www.statcan.gc.ca/daily-quotidien/070502/t070502c-eng.htm

Canadian Teachers' Federation (2006). Commercialism in Canadian schools: who's calling the shots. Canadian Teachers' Federation, Canadian Centre for Policy Alternatives

Casper LM, McLanahan SS, Garfinkel I (1994) The gender poverty gap: what we can learn from other countries. Am Sociol Rev 59:594–605

Caston RJ (1998) Life in a business-oriented society: a sociological perspective. Allyn and Bacon, Boston

Community Foundations of Canada (2010) Canada's vital signs 2010. Community Foundations of Canada

Côté JE, Allahar AL (2006) Critical youth studies: a Canadian focus. Pearson Prentice Hall, Toronto

Durrant JE (2000) Trends in youth crime and well-being since the abolition of corporal punishment in Sweden. Youth Soc 31(4):437

Ehrenreich B (1990) Fear of falling: the inner life of the middle class. Harper Perennial, New York

Eisler L, Schissel B (2008) Globalization, justice and the demonization of youth. Int J Soc Inquiry 1(1):167–187

Elementary Teachers Federation of Ontario (2008) Full-day kindergarten: moving Ontario forward. Elementary Teachers Federation of Ontario

Eshleman JR (1997) The family. Allyn and Bacon, Boston

Finnie R (1993) Women, men and the economic consequences of divorce: evidence from Canadian longitudinal data. Can Rev Sociol Anthropol 30(2):205–241

Giroux HA (2004) The terror of neoliberalism: authoritarianism and the eclipse of democracy. Paradigm, Boulder

Giroux HA (2009) Youth in a suspect society: democracy or disposability? Palgrave Macmillan, New York

Harvey D (2010) The enigma of capital: and the crises of capitalism. Oxford University Press, USA

Health Canada (2002) A report on mental illnesses in Canada. Health Canada Editorial Board Mental Illnesses, Canada

Health Canada (2003) Report on the workshop on suicide-related research in Canada. Health Canada, Ottawa

Hurst M (2011) Debt and family type in Canada. Statistics Canada, Ottawa

Jacobson J, Saville E (1999) Neighbourhood warden schemes: an overview. Great Britain home office, policing and reducing crime unit research, development and statistics directorate

Jamieson W, Hart L (2003) Compendium of promising crime prevention practices in Canada. Caledon Institute of Social Policy, Ottawa

Jarjoura GR, Triplett RA, Brinker GP (2002) Growing up poor: examining the link between persistent childhood poverty and delinquency. J Quant Criminol 18(2):159–187

Jenson J (2003) Young families, social risk and the role of government: analysis and recommendations for Ontario. Canadian Policy Research Networks, Ottawa

Juby H, Farrington DP (2001) Disentangling the link between disrupted families and delinquency. Br J Criminol 41(1):22

Katz J (1988) Seductions of crime: moral and sensual attractions in doing evil. Basic Books, New York

Lambert M, Zeman K, Allen M, Bussiere P (2004) Who pursues postsecondary education, who leaves and why: results from the youth in transition survey. Culture, Tourism and the Centre for Education Statistics Division, Statistics Canada

Lochner L, Moretti E (2001) The effect of education on crime: evidence from prison inmates, arrests, and self-reports. National Bureau of Economic Research Cambridge, Cambridge

Muncie J (2006) Governing young people: coherence and contradiction in contemporary youth justice. Crit Soc Pol 26(4):770–793

Petersen AC, Mortimer JT (1994) Youth unemployment and society. Cambridge University Press, Cambridge

Rehnby N, McBride S (1997) Help wanted: economic security for youth. Canadian Centre for Policy Alternatives

Scott MS, United States Department of Justice, Office of Community Oriented Policing Services (2002) Disorderly youth in public places. United States Department of Justice, Office of Community Oriented Policing Services

Smock PJ (1993) The economic costs of marital disruption for young women over the past two decades. Demography 30:353–371

Smock PJ (1994) Gender and the short-run economic consequences of marital disruption. Soc Forces 73:243–262

Stanford J (2011) Having their cake and eating it too. Canadian Centre For Policy Alternatives

Straus MA, Sugarman DB, Giles-Sims J (1997) Spanking by parents and subsequent antisocial behavior of children. Arch Pediatr Adolesc Med 151(8):761

Taylor I (1999) Crime in context: a critical criminology of market societies. Westview, Boulder

Taylor CA, Manganello JA, Lee SJ, ice JC (2010) Mothers' spanking of 3-year-old children and subsequent risk of children's aggressive behavior. Pediatrics 125(5):e1057

Therborn, G (2011) The world: a beginner' guide. Polity, Cambridge

Thomas EM (2009) Canadian nine-year-olds at school. Statistics Canada

Turner SM (2002) Something to cry about: an argument against corporal punishment of children in Canada. Wilfrid Laurier University Press, Waterloo

Unicef (2009) Canadian supplement to the state of the world's children 2009. Canadian Unicef Committee

Wells LE, Ranken JH (1991) Families and delinquency: a meta-analysis of the impact of broken homes. Soc Problems 38:71–93

White RD, Wyn J, Albanese P (2011) Youth and society: exploring the social dynamics of youth experience. Oxford University Press, Oxford

Willms JD (2002) Vulnerable children: findings from Canada's national longitudinal survey. University of Alberta Press, Edmonton

Yalnizyan A (2009) Exposed: revealing truths about Canada's recession. Canadian Centre for Policy Alternatives

Yalnizyan A (2010) The problem of poverty post-recession. Canadian Centre for Policy Alternatives

Young J (2007a) Slipping away-moral panics each side of 'the golden age'. In: Downes D, Cohen S, Rock P, Chinkin C (eds) Crime, social control and human rights. Willan, Devon, pp 53–64

Young J (2007b) The vertigo of late modernity. Sage, London

Chapter 3
The Nature of Youth Crime

Abstract This chapter examines some important aspects of what we know about the quality and quantity of youth crime. One of the key arguments is that there are severe limitations associated with official sources of data for certain types of crimes, thus reducing our confidence in fully understanding the nature and level of youth crime in Canada. Keeping these limitations in mind, the chapter shows that youth are not getting more violent and that a significant contributor to the perception of increased youth violence lies in the category of common assault which is sensitive to changes in official responses to youths behavior. The chapter also examines the relevance of categories such as "race," class, and gender.

If we are to develop and implement effective youth criminal justice and social policies, we need to know as accurately as possible, exactly what we are dealing with. Not only do we need to understand the social context in which many youth live (the focus of Chap. 2) and how many youth commit crimes, we also need to understand what kinds of crimes they perpetrate, and the characteristics of the youth who commit them. In other words, we need an understanding of the qualitative and quantitative dimensions of youth crime. But these tasks are easier contemplated than accomplished. For a host of methodological and ideological reasons, as well as reasons emanating from the presentation of crime by the media to the public, we know much less about youth crime than we could. In this chapter, I want to take up some explanations for this, beginning with methodological questions relating to how we count crime, and what we count.

The Advantages and Dangers of Statistics

In a scathing critique of the "numbers game," in Criminology, Jock Young (2004, p. 13) argues that

> We are confronted at this moment with an orthodox criminology which is denatured and desiccated. Its actors inhabit an arid planet where they are either driven into crime by

S. Alvi, *Youth Criminal Justice Policy in Canada*, SpringerBriefs in Criminology,   49
DOI: 10.1007/978-1-4419-0273-3_3, © The Author(s) 2012

social and psychological deficits or make opportunistic choices in the criminal market-place....They are, furthermore, digital creatures of quantity, they obey probabilistic laws of deviancy—they can be represented by the statistical symbolism of lambda, chi and sigma, their behaviour can be captured in the intricacies of regression analysis and equation.

Young's point is that orthodox positivist (or mainstream) criminology has for too long cleaved to the idea that only statistical analysis can provide us with the truth about crime, which in turn assumes that crime can actually be measured accurately in the first place. Along with Young, I do not wish to throw out the statistical "baby with the bathwater." As he cautions, we should not declare "open season" on numbers because in fact, some numbers are "indispensible" for sociological analysis. Homicide data for instance are one of the more useful and accurate criminal behavior indicators because they are not as susceptible to errors of non-reporting as other crimes, such as theft (Daly and Wilson 1988). Other numbers, however, are prone to error, and at the very least should be used with caution. Young opines:

> There are things in the social landscape which are distinct, definite and measurable, there are many others that are blurred because we do not know them—some because we are unlikely ever to know them, others, more importantly, which are blurred because it is their nature to be blurred. Precision must be constantly eyed with suspicion, decimal points with raised eyebrows. There are very many cases where statistical testing is inappropriate because the data is technically weak—it will simply not bear the weight of such analysis. There are many other instances where the data is blurred and contested and where such testing is simply wrong (Young 2004, p. 22).

Imagine being asked to publicly comment on an alleged "tremendous increase" in juvenile crime in your city or town. Before giving an answer, what issues would have to be thought through? Assume that the questioner presents us with the "startling" statistical fact that violent juvenile crime has doubled in the past year. What would we have to know before commenting on this apparently dramatic upsurge? Now consider a few additional pieces of information in this hypothetical situation; we know that there were two violent criminal incidents involving youth last year and four this year, but in addition, the way police respond to violent incidents has changed due to new laws, and the five largest businesses in your community have laid off thousands of employees in the past 12 months. What remarks would we make now?

Those confronted with statistics generally fall into two categories. Many hold the belief that in addition to (or perhaps because of) being complicated and too difficult to learn, statistics are a modern day form of voodoo, or a violation of "common sense." Others feel that statistics are equivalent to "scientific truth." As Hagan (Hagan 1997) points out, when people agree with a particular statistical finding, they often consider such findings to be "obvious" whereas if they disagree, they view the findings as unscientific because "common sense" tells them so.

The example above illustrates the importance of understanding both the strengths and limitations of claims based on empirical data. In answering the question posed in the example, an important piece of information is that there were two incidents last year, but two more this year. Mathematically speaking, this does represent a doubling of one type of juvenile violent crime. However, the extent to which this type of crime is a problem—two incidents versus four—is not as grave as the term "doubling" suggests. More important, drawing conclusions solely on the basis of the numbers leaves us with very little information on the causes of the increase. Of course, a proper interpretation of statistics in this example would require pointing out the practical and real world significance of the term "doubling." Careful analysis and interpretation of data to drive social policies are crucial, but should also include careful consideration of the context in which crime occurs.

Thus, although part of understanding and acting on a social phenomenon such as youth crime requires knowledge of the statistics pertaining to that phenomenon, it also requires some understanding of the strengths and limitations of the ways we gather data and how we interpret them. Before delving into the numbers on youth crime in Canada, we will briefly consider some of the strong points and hazards involved in counting youth crime.

Counting Crime

There are basically only a few ways that we can count crime. *Official statistics* are derived from what authorities such as the police, the courts or probation workers tell us about crime. Through *victimization surveys* we can ask people how often and the circumstances in which they have been victimized by crime. Using *self report surveys* we can ask people how often and the circumstances associated with crimes they have committed. By using *observational techniques* we can gain valuable information about crime by observing from a distance or even participating in an environment in which crime occurs. Each of these approaches has their advantages and limitations, as follows.

Official Data

Most of the data on youth crime used in this book are official statistics—those deriving from the police through the Uniform Crime Reporting Survey (UCR), as well as judicial and correctional sources. These data are not necessarily the best sources of statistical information on youth crime, but they tend to be the only kinds of reasonably comprehensive data on youth crime available in Canada. The UCR is a yearly national survey that counts the number of "criminal code and other statute offences reported to the police across Canada" (Canadian Centre for Justice Statistics 1998). These data under-represent less serious offences because when a person is charged with more than one offence, only the most serious one is counted. As well, these official data only reflect those cases that have come to the attention of police and where charges have been laid. This means that factors such as police discretion (e.g., the decision not to lay charges or to divert youth from the system under Extra-Judicial measures), the willingness of victims to report a crime, and changes in the definition of crime all play a role in restricting our knowledge of the exact number and types of crimes committed by youth. The revised Uniform Crime Reporting Survey (or UCR2) was developed in the mid 1990s and is non-representative data collected from mostly urban police departments in various provinces. It collects information on incidents reported to the police but also includes information on age, sex, relationship of the accused and victim, location of the incident, presence of weapon, and degree of injury to the victim. In 2004, a new version, the UCR 2.2, was introduced to account for crimes that had not been counted in the past, such as hate crime or cyber crime. Another recent development has seen the introduction of the Crime Severity Index (CSI), which measures changes in the severity of crime based on the level of sentencing handed down by courts for each criminal incident. The first reporting of data on the CSI for youth was released by Statistics Canada in 2010.

Judicial sources of data derive from the Youth Court Survey which provides information on the number of cases heard in youth courts. Each case consists of all charges laid against the individual under federal statute (e.g., the Criminal Code of Canada). Corrections data count the number of young persons who are remanded in custody, in temporary detention or who have been sentenced to a correctional facility. The most important problem with these data is that they are "post hoc," that is, they only tell us about those youth who have already been caught and processed by the system. Indeed, official data tell us more about the activities of official agencies than they tell us about actual crime levels. Nevertheless due to the absence of comprehensive and long-term data from other sources, I will need to utilize official data in this book. Where possible, however, I draw upon statistical and qualitative data from other sources.

Victimization Surveys

Originally intended to reflect a relatively new focus on the concerns of victims of crime, victimization surveys are designed to determine the number and nature of crimes which are often not reported to the police. They do so by asking people to report on the nature of their experiences with crime. In Canada, government sponsored surveys such as the General Social Survey are carried out every 5 years, and only tap victimizations of households and individuals. Thus, many crimes against institutions, such as department stores are excluded. The central problem with this technique, however, is that it tends to under-report crime because survey respondents often forget when, or may not even know if they have been victimized, are sometimes unable to determine whether they have actually been victimized by a criminal offence and may not report for fear of reprisal or other negative consequences if they report being victimized. Particularly important for our purposes, it is often difficult for victims of crime to determine whether the perpetrator was a youth or not, especially if the crime has been a property crime such as theft or break and enter (Doob et al. 1998).

Self-Report Studies

Self-report studies attempt to determine the amount of crime that exists by asking people to admit to committing various criminal acts through the use of anonymous surveys for example.

The main goal of these non-official methods of counting crime is to eliminate as much as possible the "interference" associated with official data gathering techniques. This is because official crime data such as those available from the Uniform Crime Reports (UCR) or court statistics, only measure the extent to which these authorities process crime. As pointed out earlier, official data really measure police or court activity rather than the number of actual crimes occurring in a community. Thus, self-report studies ask people who may, or may not have encountered the criminal justice system whether they have ever committed an offence in the hopes that they will answer honestly about their behavior. Of course, the main difficulty with this method is that people may forget what offences they committed and when they did them, or they may lie because they do not want to admit that they committed a crime. As well, because it would be expensive and logistically difficult to survey everyone, self-report surveys must rely on accurate sampling procedures so that their results may be generalized to the larger population. Unfortunately, however, studies of crime using this method have often surveyed "atypical" samples, thereby limiting the extent to which they can claim relevance to the entire population (Hagan 1997). Moreover, with a few exceptions, (Lagier 1982; McCarthy and Hoge 1984; Haapasalo and Tremblay 1994) Canadian self-report surveys of youth crime are relatively rare.

Data from Observations

Observing "crime in the making" allows researchers to gain a somewhat different perspective on crime than that allowed by the methods above. Such "observational" research generally falls into two categories; the researcher can watch and record criminal activity from a distance and does not disturb the social setting (field observation), or researchers can interact with the people they wish to understand either by participating completely in the activities of interest (participant observation) or by observing as a participant to the extent that the participants themselves allow it (observer as participant). Indeed, one of the strengths of gathering data from observation is that it provides information which might be difficult to collect using traditional techniques such as surveys or interviews. For example, we may gain some insight into the dynamics of youth gangs by interviewing a few gang members or even administering a questionnaire (Venkatesh 1997). However, researchers are likely to gain new and different insights if they actually watch how the gang members interact with one another, observe how authority relationships are played out, or monitor how particular rituals are conducted. In effect, observing how a subculture performs has the potential to provide very useful information. Thus, observational data help us to understand other, more qualitative dimensions of criminal activity. However, such methods and the data they produce are vulnerable to the subjective interpretations of the researcher although careful research designs can mitigate this problem. As well, it is often difficult or dangerous to gain access to the people being studied as well as their trust, as many such individuals are suspicious of the motives of researchers.

Other Problems with Data on Youth Crime

Several other "crime counting" issues warrant attention. A significant one in Canada is that official data sources do not provide comprehensive information on the "race" or ethnic background of those processed by the criminal justice system. One of the main arguments of those critical of contemporary criminal justice strategies in Canada is that the system is biased against particular minority groups. As we shall see, this claim has some validity despite the fact that there are very few studies examining racial discrimination in the Canadian criminal justice system (Wortley 1999; Roberts 2002; Wortley 2003). Others, however, contend that the system is not "racist," that it functions according to principles of equality, and that any disproportional representation of particular minorities is related to the qualities of those individuals (Wilson and Herrnstein 1985).

A keystone of the debate is that it is scientifically impossible to classify people according to race. The concept of "race" is dated and in fact is not used by many social scientists any longer. This is because genetically, human beings cannot be divided into discrete categories based on biological properties, and indeed, human beings share 99.9% of their genes (Rex 1983; Zack 2001). However, although we all belong to one, "human race," our society (along with many others) most certainly contains individuals and institutions that racialize other people. Accordingly, while we can talk meaningfully about *racism* and the fact that aspects of human behavior are often *racialized*, technically, the concept of race is virtually useless. Thus, collecting crime statistics which include race involves an acute understanding of the methodological problems involved in operationalizing racial categories, and balancing knowledge of the degree to which the criminal justice system is racist (in terms of the way police or courts act toward people of color for instance) with the potential stereotyping that might also arise when particular groups are singled out as being over-represented in the system because they are supposedly genetically predisposed to crime (see Box 3.1).

Gabor (1994), who has commented extensively on the race-crime data debate, draws our attention to some additional points:

- Differences in crime rates vary more within racial groups than they do between them. Collecting race data will therefore distract from what should be the real focus of concern.
- Any racial differences in crime rates could be the result of the discriminatory practices of criminal justice personnel such as police, judges, and prosecutors. By collecting data on race and crime, our understanding of the intersection of race and crime will not only be improved, it will bring the issue into the open. Open discussion is preferable to the negative stereotyping that tends to occur when people have few facts.
- Even if we did find links between race and crime, what could we do about it? Unlike poverty, "race" is a characteristic we can do nothing about. On the other hand, the criminal justice system already collects data on factors such as age and sex over which we have no control.

Another issue unique to the Canadian context is that official charge rates may be sensitive to the rate at which young people are not charged under the YCJA. Put differently, the existence of Extra-judicial measures means that some youth who commit offences may not be formally charged, or may be dealt with informally (e.g., when police give a warning or discuss the incident with the youth's parents). Data on youth not charged from several jurisdictions in Canada show that the rate of youth not charged has been increasing since the late 1990s, ranging between 37 and 44% in the period 1997 and 2002, and rising sharply after implementation of the YCJA in 2003, where it currently remains stable at approximately 60% (Taylor-Butts and Bressan 2008). On the face it, these data seem to indicate that there has been a gradual movement towards not charging youth for violations, but there are still things that we do not know. For instance, we do not know how accurate these data are because police (who are responsible for exercising the discretion required as to whether to charge a youth or not), may not be accurately recording "not charged" incidents, since it is more important to them that they accurately record charges (Carrington and Schulenberg 2005). As Carrington and Schulenberg (2005, p. 9) also point out, we do not know with certainty the extent to which non-charges go hand in hand with net-widening, where an increase in the number of youth who are subjected to extra-judicial measures exceeds a decrease in the number of youth charged, which might mean an increase in the number of youth apprehended by police, or, the extent to which extra-judicial measures might involve formal cautions and referrals, versus taking no action or providing informal warnings.

A further gap in our empirical knowledge of youth crime concerns our lack of knowledge of the number and type of certain *kinds* of crimes being committed by youth. For example, while we know something about the kinds of *hate crimes* that are perpetrated in Canada, we have very little information on the extent to which youth under 18 are the perpetrators.

In addition, consider the matter of female crime and victimization. It is well known that women's experiences in relation to crime have traditionally been ignored in mainstream criminology, owing to a perception that the level and seriousness of crimes committed by women are trivial or insignificant. Generally, even those accounts which purport to take account of gender are characterized by an "add women and stir" approach which ignores the *gendered* nature of women's and men's lives. In other words, approaches that simply break up aggregate data into categories that tell us "how many" males and females were victims or perpetrators disregard the different *consequences* and *experiences* of male and female young offenders in both coming to, and being in the criminal justice system. In short, simply pulling out data on males versus females assumes, incorrectly, that male and female offenders are the same except for their sex. For example, although most would agree that youth prostitution is problematic, we do not know precisely how many young boys and girls are engaged in this activity in Canada, nor should we forget that most *adult* female prostitutes began their careers when they were juveniles. Furthermore while we understand something about the nature of youth gangs in Canada, we know next to nothing about the role and experiences of females in such groups (Esbensen and Winfree 1998). Simply discussing "how many" girls and boys participate in gangs or prostitution tells us little of the "lived experiences" of these individuals. In terms of gang activity, there is a definitional issue at the core of the lack of statistical data on such groups, namely, what is a youth gang? There are big differences between actual gang activity and groups of unsupervised youth "hanging out" and perhaps getting into trouble together. Further, youth gangs vary greatly in terms of their composition and the kinds of activities they carry out (Bala 1997; Laidler and Hunt 2001), and this often complicates our ability to provide detailed statistical profiles and analyses of such groups.

Another problem is that with the exception of a few case studies (Hagan and McCarthy 1997; Baron and Hartnagel 2002; Gaetz 2004) we have virtually no Canadian national data on the characteristics and experiences of *street* youth, such as their family backgrounds, patterns of criminality, school problems, and unemployment history. This is a particularly important gap in our knowledge of youth crime as data from these studies have indicated not only that there are increasing numbers of homeless in Canada, but that many homeless youth are both the victims and perpetrators of large amounts of criminal activity.

To summarize, then, we have seen that there are important strengths and limitations associated with the kinds of data we have on crime in general and youth crime in particular. Indeed, these limitations have prompted many to call for a "data triangulation" strategy of gathering crime data which combines several of the techniques discussed above to obtain a more rounded or "more substantive picture of reality" (Berg 1995). Overall, relying only on one method of gathering data contributes to what criminologists have called the "dark" or "hidden" figure of crime—a term referring to the reality that such methods almost always underrepresent actual levels of crime.

We have also seen that there is much we do not know about youth crime (or adult crime for that matter) in relation to "race" or ethnicity and gender. Keeping in mind the limitations we have discussed so far, we will now examine data on the nature and levels of youth crime, and the characteristics of youth who commit them.

Box 3.1. In this Robbery, Race was not Relevant

October 17, 1998
    Don Sellar, Toronto Star
    A FEW hours after the holdup at the City Savings and Credit Union Ltd. in North York, the police issued a news release that described three suspects.
    Here they are:
    Suspect #1: Male/black, mid-1920s, 6 ft. 1 in., slim build, wearing a light green army style jacket, black mask, dark pants, purple sunglasses. Armed with a long-barrel rifle.
    Suspect #2: Male/black, early 1920s, 5 ft. 8 in.–5 ft. 10 in., average build but stockier than #1, wearing black 3/4-length jacket, black pants, black mask and dark sunglasses. He was armed with a black handgun.
    Suspect #3: Male/black, 25–30 years, black short dreadlock hair, wearing a green army fatigue mask with a black hat. This suspect was driving a stolen red Chrysler Caravan licence 863 YWP.
    Next day, The Star on Page A24 ran a concise 250-word story about the robbery, one in which no shots were fired but staff were advised to hurry up with the cash—or else.
    The aftermath of this robbery seemed like something out of The Gang That Couldn't Shoot Straight. Suspects #1 and #2 ran away with an undisclosed amount of money, but couldn't find their getaway car and wheelman, Suspect #3.
    When the gun-toting duo tried to steal a car in the nearby neighbourhood, they were twice outwitted. First, they were unable to con two children into getting mom out of the house so that she could be robbed of the family car. Next, they tried to force a woman from her van at gunpoint, but she sped away unhurt.
    On the third try, they grabbed a 1988 white Pontiac 6000, whose 67-year-old owner acquiesced only after being hit in the face with a gun butt.
    "Police are looking for three men," The Star's story ended, laconically.
    "Do you not think that this crime is vicious and callous and serious enough to provide a full description of the people involved?" a reader asked the Bureau of Accuracy.
    "The radio stations and other papers indicate they are black, but The Star in its political correctness describes the suspect as police looking for three men. If this ludicrous policy doesn't change, I'll be cancelling my subscription," the man said.
    "When they're black, they're black, and it should be stated so in the paper," a second caller said. "How in the dickens are you going to find these people without the proper descriptions?"
    What did other papers do?

A check of The Globe and Mail revealed that Canada's national paper was otherwise engaged. No story.

The tabloid Sun devoted nearly a page to the crime—Kids, granny foil thugs;

Fleeing bank robbers on carjack terror reign—and reported the suspects' race.

In my view, there was little point in doing so. The descriptions were hopelessly vague. They fitted thousands of young black men in Canada's largest city. Two of the suspects wore masks.

By the time the paper came out the next day, unless the holdup men were vying for the "stupid crooks" feature in Ann Landers' column, they could easily have changed clothes and licence plates.

Frankly, the chance of a reader turning in this trio of crooks on such flimsy descriptions seems so slight that it isn't worth the risk of branding thousands of law-abiding black men as potential criminals.

So The Star's sensible policy of not reporting a person's race, colour or religion "unless it is pertinent to the story" must be applied in this case.

It doesn't always. The policy is flexible enough to allow race or colour to be reported, say, when a detailed suspect description is available or grave danger exists. If the crook has a scar across the left cheek or a remarkable tattoo, his race might be the clincher.

Once an arrest is made, there is usually less justification for injecting race into the story. An exception might be when police shoot a criminal suspect and the issue of racial motivation is being hotly debated.

But to those who periodically tell a news ombud that race is an essential ingredient in defining the criminal classes—or, "I want to know who I should be afraid of"—sorry, I can not buy those arguments.

The Magnitude and Nature of Youth Crime

Most studies show that almost every young person in Canada has committed some kind of delinquent act (Doob et al. 1998), but that the vast majority of crimes committed by young people are minor (Doob and Cesaroni 2004). In a study of 3,000 youth in Montreal, for instance, Leblanc (1983) found that 90% of youth had committed a crime. Another study of Toronto youth reported that less than half of youth who had reported that they had committed some kind of delinquent act in their lifetime were caught by authority figures (Savoie 2007). Similarly, West (1984) used self-report data to show that over 90% of Canadian-high school boys had committed some "deviant" act such as swearing, shoplifting, drinking, or experimenting with drugs.

If we lived in a strict law and order context governed by a law and order mentality, and assuming we could increase the efficacy of police vis-a-vis their

Table 3.1 Youths charged in selected federal statute offences, Canada, 1996–2002, by sex (rate per 100,000 youth)

Sex	Offence category	1996	1997	1998	1999	2000	2001	2002
Males	Total, criminal code offences	7506	6878.1	6599.3	6102.6	6158.6	6148.1	5797.5
Males	Violent crimes	1385.9	1321.4	1314	1256.2	1343.4	1380.7	1332.7
Males	Property crimes	4182.8	3643.6	3349.7	2957.4	2820.8	2696.6	2519.6
Males	Other criminal code offences	1937.2	1913.2	1935.6	1889	1994.4	2070.8	1945.2
Females	Total, criminal code offences	2229.7	2078.3	2049.2	1890	1952.4	2051.9	2011.1
Females	Violent crimes	451.9	473.3	475.1	444.2	480.7	507	512.1
Females	Property crimes	1256	1069.2	1003.5	905.5	899.7	911.2	900.7
Females	Other criminal code offences	521.7	535.8	570.6	540.3	572	633.8	598.4

Source Statistics Canada. Table 109-5009—Adults and youths charged, by sex and offence category, Canada, provinces and territories, annual (table), CANSIM (database), Using E-STAT (distributor)
• Violent crimes involve offences that deal with the application, or threat of application, of force to a person. These include homicide, attempted murder, various forms of sexual and non-sexual assault, robbery and abduction. Traffic incidents that result in death or bodily harm are included under Criminal Code traffic incidents
• Property crimes involve unlawful acts with the intent of gaining property but do not involve the use or threat of violence against an individual. Theft, breaking and entering, fraud, and possession of stolen goods are examples of property crimes
• Other Criminal Code offences involve the remaining offences that are not classified as violent or property crimes (excluding traffic offences). Examples are mischief, bail violations, disturbing the peace, arson, prostitution, and offensive weapons

capacity to catch offenders, then most young people in Canada would encounter the criminal justice system at some point in their lives. Thankfully, we do not live in such an environment at the moment. However, the crux of the matter is that there are big differences between so-called minor "delinquent or anti-social acts," committing a criminal offence and actually being caught or charged for that offence. In general, the incidence of minor delinquencies among most youth tends to decrease over time, and hence, a very small proportion of young people actually come into contact with the criminal justice system. In fact, in 1997, less than 5% of young Canadians were charged with a criminal offence (Canadian Centre for Justice Statistics 1998), and of these, about 5% were responsible for the majority of crimes.

In terms of overall charge rates of young offenders over time, and the type of crimes they were charged with, the data in Table 3.1 show that there has been an overall decrease in crime rates for youth since a peak that was reached in 1991. The overall decrease in the rate of youths charged with criminal offences reflects a decrease in the number of charges for *non-violent* crime, while rates of violent crime have remained relatively stable. More recent data suggests that there has been a small increase in violent youth crime as of 2006. However, it should also be

Table 3.2 Youth Accused of homicide, Canada, 1999–2009

Year	Male	Female	Rate male (per 100,000)	Rate female (per 100,000)
1999	37	9	2.92	0.75
2000	38	5	2.99	0.42
2001	27	5	2.11	0.41
2002	33	9	2.54	0.73
2003	52	10	3.96	0.83
2004	39	5	2.95	0.40
2005	62	10	4.64	0.79
2006	73	12	5.43	0.94
2007	66	8	4.93	0.63
2008	51	4	3.86	0.32
2009	73	5	5.63	0.40

Source Adapted from Beattie and Cotter (2010)

noted that much of the apparent increase in violent youth crime can be attributed to the increased tendency of youth to be involved in common (level 1) assault, which accounted for 60% of violent youth crime in 2006, and is defined by behaviors such as pushing, shoving, slapping, punching, or face-to-face fights (Taylor-Butts and Bressan 2008). Overall the trends suggest that while violent youth crime in Canada has fluctuated over the last decade, the trend remains stable because of the relatively rare occurrence of extremely violent acts such as homicide (see Table 3.2). As a recent Juristat report (Taylor-Butts and Bressan 2008, p. 3) points out:

> In 2006, both the number and rate of youth aged 12 to 17 years accused of homicide reached their highest point since data were first collected in 1961. However, just 5 years prior, the youth homicide rate was at a 30-year low.

The increases in level 1 assaults may also reflect an attitude of "zero tolerance" by authority figures toward incidents and behaviors such as bullying or schoolyard fighting that in the past might have been seen as somewhat "normal" and therefore subject to informal resolutions (Tanner 1996; Bala 1997; Schissel 1997). As one scholar points out the reality is that "the vast majority of assaults are minor and do not cause bodily harm" (Reitsma-Street 1993). This does not mean, however, that they do not cause psychological or emotional damage, but the point is that *official responses* to such incidents have changed in that there is a greater chance today that such behaviors will be criminalized.

If we look at trends by category of crime since 1997, youth crime has generally decreased in terms of offences like sexual assault, theft under and over $5,000, shoplifting and fraud, but increased in terms of most drug offences, mischief, and disturbing the peace (see Table 3.3). Again, with respect to violent crimes, it should be kept in mind that base rates are low to begin with, and therefore, the apparent percentage increase in violent crimes such as homicide and counterfeiting currency are not as dramatic as they seem. Rather, it is in the categories of

Table 3.3 Percent change in total youth crime rate 1997–2006 by offence

	Percent change
Homicide	41
Attempted murder	6
Assault—total	*17*
Level 1	11
Level 2—weapon	40
Level 3—aggravated	21
Other assaults—total	*13*
Unlawfully causing bodily harm	−86
Discharge firearm with intent	28
Assault against police	97
Assault against other peace-public officers	17
Other assaults	−17
Sexual assault—total	*−8*
Level 1	−6
Level 2—weapon	−53
Level 3—aggravated	−70
Other sexual offences	1
Abduction	−5
Robbery	−2
Violent crime—total	*12*
Breaking and entering	−47
Motor vehicle theft	−41
Theft over $5,000	−61
Theft $5,000 and under—total	*−33*
Shoplifting	−46
Other	−7
Possession of stolen goods	9
Fraud	−24
Property crime—total	*−34*
Mischief	46
Counterfeiting currency	39
Bail violations	33
Disturbing the peace	217
Offensive weapons	44
Prostitution	−81
Arson	1
Kidnapping/forcible confinement	66
Other	−3
Other Criminal Code offences—total	*34*
Criminal Code—total (excluding traffic)	−6
Drug offences—total	*97*
Heroin	−54
Cocaine	135
Other drugs	156
Cannabis	91

Source Adapted from Taylor-Butts and Bressan (2008), p. 11

relatively minor offences, particularly "disturbing the peace" that we see the more important shifts.

With respect to property crimes, despite a few minor increases between 1987 and 1997, rates have generally decreased since 1997. Administration of justice offences, which include failure to appear in court, breaching of probation orders or failing to comply with an order, have also decreased by 11% since 2002/2003 (Milligan 2010). In addition, charges levied against young persons for drug violations have also increased, despite the fact that criminalizing drug use has done little, historically, to curb drug use (Currie 1993; Jensen et al. 2004).

Finally, for the first time in Canada we have reported data on the severity of youth crime. Since 2001, these data suggest that the severity of violent crime has generally been declining since 2001 (Dauvergne and Turner 2010).

Thus, the *vast majority* of charges laid against youth involve non-violent offences. Property crime accounts for 4 out of 10 charges laid, while about one-quarter of all charges fall into the "other" category. Only about one in four of all charges laid involves violence but as noted many of these offences were driven by increases in assault, most of which are Level 1 offences. More important in light of media driven perceptions of extremely violent youth, homicide made up less than 0.05% of all charges laid in 2006. Further, the Canadian Centre for Justice Statistics reports that in 80% of charges of violent crime in 2006, no weapon was used, while a firearm was used in 14% of cases (Taylor-Butts and Bressan 2008). Again, the point here is not to trivialize those incidents in which severe force or harm to victims was involved, but to illustrate the reality of youth crime as distinct from media accounts and popular images.

Tracking charge rates *prior* to the implementation of the Young Offenders Act in 1984 provides one more instructive insight. Schissel observes that soon after the Young Offenders Act was enforced, youth crime rates "were driven upward, almost in a linear fashion," and that while some of the initial increases can be attributed to the YOA's inclusion of 17- and 18-year-olds, the shifts cannot be explained by actual increases in crime, particularly in light of the remarkable coincidence between higher charge rates and the implementation of the Act (Schissel 1997, p. 75). He also points out that the use of informal, diversionary ways of dealing with youth transgressions—a central principle of the Young Offenders Act as laid out in section 4—did not grow proportionately with the increase in formal approaches. He has concluded that the spirit of the Young Offenders Act was being violated (Schissel 1993). In effect, a good deal of what we know about youth crime from official data such as these underlines the view that variations in crime rates are a function of law making and law enforcement practices (Carrington and Moyer 1994). It is probably too early to tell in what ways the changing legislative landscape as crystallized in the YCJA will impact on young offenders, and as discussed earlier, the YCJA itself may change in some fundamental ways very soon.

In terms of sentencing, since the implementation of the YCJA, the number of youth receiving custodial sentences has declined from 27% of all cases in 2002/2003 to 17% in 2006/2007 (Thomas 2008). Table 3.4 illustrates the percent change in

Table 3.4 Percent change in rates of youth admitted to correctional services from 2008/2009, 2004/2005, and 2007/2008

	Percent change in rate from 2004/2005 to 2008/2009	Percent change in rate from 2007/2008 to 2008/2009
Custodial supervision		
Sentenced to custody	−27.8	−2.7
Secure custody	−29.0	−0.4
Open custody	−26.4	−5.1
Remand	−4.5	−5.5
Total custodial supervision	−10.1	−4.9
Community supervision		
Probation	a	−1.2
Selected YCJA sentences		
Community portion of a custody and supervision order	a	−10.4
Deferred custody and supervision order	a	2.0
Intensive support and supervision	a	17.0
Total community supervision		−1.6
Total correctional services		−3.2

Source Adapted from (Calverley et al. 2010, p. 19)

[a] Since admissions to YCJA sentences for British Columbia are included in the probations category for 2004/2005, the number of admissions to probation and to the YCJA sentences in 2008/2009 cannot be compared to 2004/2005

youth admitted to correctional services between 2004/2005, and 2007/2008. The data suggests that with the exception of Intensive Support and Supervision (ISSP)—a new sentencing provision under the YCJA similar to probation but with closer support and supervision—and deferred custody—also a new sentencing option allowing the offender to serve the sentence in the community under strict conditions—there has been a decline in all other sentence rates.

This increased reliance on communities to provide supervision and rehabilitation services for young people may be problematic, given that increasingly, community resources are not available, have been cut, or in some cases, funding for programs are on a pilot, rather than ongoing basis. The John Howard society noted that there is also a great deal of variation in the types of programs that are available for youth sentenced to an ISSP, with some being very controversial and even invasive (e.g., bootcamps), thereby requiring the informed and voluntary consent of the young offender (John Howard Society of Canada 2000). Indeed, these realities may help to explain why Intensive Support and Supervision orders are an "opt-in" sanction under the YCJA, meaning that provinces and territories can choose to opt out of this provision if there are no community resources available to address service needs (Thomas 2008). As Bala et al. (2009, p. 149) point out:

Although significant efforts have been made to establish these services in all provinces, there has been very little recorded use of the sentence of intensive supervision and support outside of British Columbia. Of the 347 recorded sentences of intensive supervision and support in Canada in 2006/2007, 301 were in British Columbia.

Thus, in the context of devolution of financial responsibility to communities, and in the shadow of the recent recession, it remains to be seen whether alternatives to incarceration for young offenders can even be sustained over the coming years let alone increased. While funds have been allocated for preventative measures and government/community partnerships in the most recent Federal budget, the funding commitment is only for 2 years (Carrington and Shulenberg 2005; Canadian Coalition for the Rights of Children 2011). Certainly, if cuts to service agencies are made in Canada, and if youth continue to be "responsibilized" to cooperate with communities to achieve successful reintegration into those communities, then the experiences of the UK may be instructive (see Box 3.2).

Box 3.2: Public Sector Cuts: Rise in Youth Crime Feared as Key Teams are Reduced

Ministers told that councils will find it 'exceptionally difficult to maintain a basic youth offending team'
Alan Travis

- The Guardian, Friday 25 March 2011

White Gold project, Redruth
Cut: £185,000

A crime prevention project in Cornwall that has helped more than 960 young people since it started in 2003 is to close at the end of this month because its £185,000 funding from a government local area agreement is to end. The project, White Gold, a partnership between the police and Cornwall youth offending team (YOT), is an early casualty of funding cuts.

Nationally, ministers have been warned that funding reductions will mean that some of the 157 local authorities across England and Wales will find it "exceptionally difficult to maintain a basic youth offending team". Sandwell council in the West Midlands has placed the entire 80-strong YOT staff on its "at risk of redundancy register", as cuts of up to 30% in youth justice funding start to bite across England and Wales.

The national network of YOTs was set up to bring together the work of the police, probation, social services, education and others in tackling youth offending, with significant results in cutting crime, which council leaders now fear will rise.

The decision by Sandwell follows 3 years in which the number of young people in the borough entering the criminal justice system dropped by 400—more than 60%.

> Councillor Derek Rowley said: "The severity of these forced cuts from central government, coupled with the fact that it has yet to confirm significant other funding, has left us with no choice but to put all staff in the service 'at risk'. Even if the funding is forthcoming, we are still facing about a 25–30% reduction on last year's budget."
>
> YOTs were told this year to expect a 10% cut in their Whitehall funding—which accounts for about a third of their resources—but have just been told this is being doubled to 20%.
>
> London councils have written to ministers warning that cuts of up to 30% in the capital will set back efforts to reduce teenage crime. Hounslow YOT faces a 32% cut in its Whitehall funding, Enfield a 31% cut and Barnet a 28% reduction. They said that giving them only one month's notice before the new allocations came into effect at the end of this month was "not acceptable".
>
> guardian.co.uk © Guardian News and Media Limited 2011

Gender

One other point should be made here regarding the data presented in Tables 3.1 and 3.2. It is that gender remains by far the most significant predictor of youth (and adult) crime. Indeed, violent youth crime is overwhelmingly committed by males a fact which directly undermines the oft-heard and increasingly tiresome argument that women (young or old) are as violent as men. Moreover, according to Mahony (2011, p. 19), in 2009:

> Females accounted for more than one quarter (28%) of youth (under 18 years of age) accused by police and more than one fifth (22%) of adult accused...
>
> Female youth crime rates were, on average, triple those of adult women. For example, rates of assault level 1 were 579 per 100,000 female youth compared to 190 per 100,000 adult females. Rates of female youth offending exceeded those of female adults across all offence categories, with the exception of homicide or other violations causing death, fraud, traffic violations, and prostitution.

The most common offences for female youth in 2009 were theft under $5,000, Level 1 assault, administration of justice violations, mischief, drug offences, and uttering threats. As noted earlier, it is important to remember that the increase in assaults is likely related to lower tolerance of bullying, schoolyard fighting, and the like. But we should also take note that there seems to be less tolerance of this kind of behavior among females than males, given that charges in the category of common assault for females tripled between 1987 and 1997 (Canadian Centre for Justice Statistics 1998), while charges for males doubled over that decade. In other words, if charge rates are a reflection of the effectiveness of policing, then boys and girls may well be being policed differently, at least when it comes to common assault.

As we saw earlier, crime rates have been declining for both males and females, but the rate of decline more recently is more pronounced for males. Male charge rates dropped from a high of 1021.8 in 1991, to 751.5 in 1997, (a decrease of 27%), while for females, the drop was from 248 in 1992 to 226.8 in 1997 (a decrease of only 7%). However, since the introduction of the YCJA, rates for females have dropped by 31%, compared to 25% for males, a trend that likely reflects the fact that females were twice as likely to commit minor theft, and that such offences are more likely to be diverted from the criminal justice system (Taylor-Butts and Bressan 2008). Moreover, female youth who are sentenced to custody often face problems because few programs are geared specifically to young women's needs (Pate 2008).

The data in these tables obscure the fact that females are more likely than males to be charged with certain kinds of offences. For instance, in 1996, Canadian police reported 165 incidents of prostitution for females, compared to just 20 for males (Juristat 1997). Once again, these figures greatly underestimate the level of actual prostitution, given the reluctance of prostitutes and their clients to reveal their activities, and the odds that some young prostitutes may be diverted from the criminal justice system toward social services agencies. Moreover, as pointed out earlier, most *adult* prostitutes start their involvement in this activity as teenagers (Lowman 1986).

Another important way in which gender matters with respect to the types of crimes young females are charged with has been highlighted by Chesney-Lind and Sheldon (1992). Using data from the United States showing that young girls who run away from home are more likely to be arrested than young boys, they maintain that young women are more likely to be charged with offences that violate taken-for-granted notions of appropriate female behavior (Tanner 1996; Chesney-Lind and Pasko 2004). In effect, although we could merely argue that there are some minor differences between the sexes in terms of the types of offences they commit, we should also be aware that these differences may also reflect different attitudes and responses of police toward young women, particularly in terms of the tendency for male police officers to act in more "chivalrous" and otherwise paternalistic ways toward women.

Race/Ethnicity and Youth Crime

As we noted earlier, there are good reasons why we do not have systematic data on the relationship between race/ethnicity and youth crime in Canada. Mosher (1996, p. 413) suggests that "Canadian research on racial discrimination in the criminal justice system is generally quite sparse," owing both to the lack of data and the false perception that Canada has not had a problem with the treatment of minority groups within the criminal justice system (Wortley 2003). Nevertheless, there are a few studies that illuminate our understanding of the link between racism and youth crime. One official source of such information comes from the Report of the Commission on Systemic Racism in the Ontario Criminal Justice System (Ontario 1995).

Table 3.5 Admissions of youths aged 16 and 17 to Ontario prisons, by sex and race, 1992/1993[a]

	Female	Male	Total
White (%)	70.8	71.9	71.8
Black (%)	1.5	13.3	12.5
Aboriginal (%)	22.0	6.3	7.5
Asian (%)	2.4	3.0	3.0
East Indian (%)	0.3	1.3	1.3
Arab (%)	0.9	0.8	0.8
Other/unknown (%)	2.1	3.3	3.2
Total Percent[a] (%)	100.0	99.9	100.1
Total Number of admissions (%)	336	4,369	4,705

Source Ontario Ministry of the Solicitor General and Correctional Services, as quoted in Report of the Commission on Systemic Racism in the Ontario Criminal Justice System (1995)
[a] Percentage estimates may not add up to 100% due to rounding

Keeping in mind that with the exception of aboriginal youth, there are no national data on charge rates for youth by race/ethnicity, data on admissions to prison for young offenders in Ontario (Table 3.5) shows at first glance that whites make up the bulk of youth incarcerated in Ontario prisons. However, when we note that groups such as aboriginals and blacks make up far less of the general population than the figures noted in this table, it is hard to disagree with the general statement that visible minorities are over-represented in the criminal justice system.

Similarly, studies conducted on the experiences of aboriginal youth consistently point to their over-representation in the criminal justice system, at every stage of the process (LaPrairie and Griffiths 1984; Morin 1990; Bala 1997).

In addition to the debates over collecting data on race/ethnic background of youth encountering the criminal justice system, we are still left with a critical question in terms of the relationship between race/ethnicity and youth crime; does over-representation indicate the racism of criminal justice officials such as police or are there links between racial and ethnic background and other factors related to criminal behavior, such as poverty and educational achievement? We know from anecdotal and court case information that police discretion plays a critical role in charges laid against visible minority youth. There is also some evidence that racism is more likely to occur at earlier stages (e.g., policing) in the criminal justice process than later (e.g., the courts) (Mosher 1996). But in addition, it is clear that some groups such as aboriginal youth are far more likely to experience high levels of economic deprivation and social isolation than their non-aboriginal counterparts. Accordingly, more definitive conclusions on the intersection of youth crime and race/ethnicity in Canada await the benefit of comprehensive, reliable and valid data. Until then, we are left with the saddening reality that groups of young people from particular "racial" and ethnic backgrounds are at considerably greater risk of being charged with offences than those belonging to dominant social groups in Canada (see Box 3.3). More recent data continues to support this contention. For example, while Aboriginal youth made up just 6% of the youth population, in 2006 they made up 27% of youth remanded in custody, 36% of those admitted to sentenced custody, and nearly a quarter (24%) of young people on probation. Moreover, this group served 3 days more on average in remand compared to their non-Aboriginal counterparts, and were more likely to be admitted for serious offences, although the length of their sentences served was approximately the same as non-Aboriginal youth (Calverley et al. 2010, p. 5). In addition, a recent study conducted by Tanner and Wortley found that while there were no differences in the rates of being stopped by police between racialized and white youth for those reporting large amounts of deviant activity, there were significant differences between these two groups of youth for those reporting no engagement in deviant behaviors, thus confirming the suspicion held by racialized minorities that "they are not equal before the law" (Tanner 2010).

The previous points are particularly salient in light of major demographic shifts that are occurring in Canada. While Canada has always been a nation of immigrants, in vivid contrast to trends going back to the 1900s and into the 1960s (when most immigrants to Canada were from Europe) the majority of immigrants to Canada today are people from the People's Republic of China, India, the Philippines, and Pakistan (Chui et al. 2007). By 2017, almost a quarter of the Canadian population will consist of visible minorities (Canada 2005), and nearly three-quarters will be living in three metropolitan areas—Toronto, Montreal, and Vancouver (Bélanger et al. 2005). Most visible minorities are a relatively young population, and nearly one-quarter are under 15. Their parents tend to be well educated, but have difficulty finding jobs in their fields. One in three lives below the poverty line (Statistics Canada 2001). And yet, we know little about the experiences of adjustment to Canadian life of newcomers to Canada, and virtually nothing about the experiences of newcomer youth. Not surprisingly, the same lack of information applies to their experiences of victimization and offending. However, the realities of demographic change will mean that more information will need to be gathered about these populations, particularly in relation to service needs, the cultural and religious competence of service providers, including those in the criminal justice system, and the role of racism in relation to immigrant youth's integration into Canadian society.

Box 3.3: Excerpted from Report of the Commission on Systemic Racism in the Ontario Criminal Justice System (1995), Chap. 6

On February 19, 1993, P, an 18-year-old black male, was stopped by the police. He and his younger brother were coming from their church's youth basketball game and were standing at Birchmount and Finch [a major intersection in Metropolitan Toronto] when a police car drove by. By way of a dare he raised his left arm, gave the peace sign and shouted "peace out, copper." The car made a U-turn and stopped in front of them. Two officers came out of the car; one white, the other Asian. The white officer approached him asked what he'd said. P explained to the officer, who then said that P had picked the wrong officer to mess with. The officer then asked him for ID [identification]. P asked if he was being arrested, and his brother pointed out that P did not have to show any ID unless he was being arrested, so P agreed with his brother not to show any ID. The next thing he knew was that he was being thrown up against the police car. There was a struggle, and the officer put handcuffs on him while P was yelling and screaming, "What's going on?" P was taken to the station, where he was charged with resisting arrest, assault, mischief and disturbing the peace. At trial, P was acquitted of all charges. The trial judge concluded that "[t]he evidence of the Crown's case through the officers suffered significantly from inconsistencies, which impacted on credibility... the overall evidence of the police left me with a distinct impression that they were overreaching, and filling in the lacunae of their case."

...A study of 248 randomly selected Youth Bureau files, drawn from completed cases at two Metropolitan Toronto police divisions, indicates that black youths are over-represented among young persons whose charges are initiated solely by the police rather than in response to a complaint. The data show that 41% of the sample as a whole, but 52% of the youths whose charges are solely initiated by the police, are black. By contrast 40% of the sample as a whole, but only 29% of youths whose charges are solely initiated by the police, are white.

Class and Youth Crime

There has been a great deal of theorizing about the relationship between class and crime. Some scholars argue that one's class position (e.g., middle or working class) has a direct association with the chances of committing a crime, being caught for one, or the type of punishment one receives, while others argue that "class doesn't matter." Much of the disagreement stems from differing theoretical understandings of the concept of class, or differing approaches in the use of data.

Like race and ethnicity, there is very little that can be said empirically in this regard as Canadian criminal justice agencies do not collect official data on the economic background of young offenders. However, Tanner (2010) points to a general pattern with respect to the relationship between class and crime—official data from the United States generally point to an inverse relationship between socio-economic status and crime (the lower the status, the higher the crime rate), while self-report data typically show no such relationship. He contends that the reasons for this difference are that self-report surveys typically involve high-school student samples, which exclude hard-core serious offenders who have dropped out of school, and that such surveys rarely ask questions about serious wrong-doing (Tanner 2010, p. 57).

In Canada, we have some data on the relationship between poverty and low-income and delinquent behaviors. For example, the National Longitudinal Survey of Canadian Youth (Canada 1996) shows that youth from lower socio-economic status are more likely to be "aggressive" than those from higher income earning groups. On the whole, however, the relationship between social class and youth crime continues to be hotly debated.

What are we to make of the seemingly contradictory conclusions about the role of economic relationships and youth crime? Again, we await good data tapping not just the offenders income levels, but also the nature of their experiences in the labor market, the extent of their under- or unemployment, and the nature of the work they do. In addition, we need to further explore the likelihood that the linkage between class and youth crime is extremely complicated, in that economic and social position is related to other factors (a *mediated* relationship) which are more directly related to crime, such as "race," gender, urbanization, the nature and availability of work, mental health, and educational attainment (Elliot and Ageton 1980; Farnworth et al. 1994; Crutchfield and Pitchford 1997; White and Cunneen 2006). Thus, the concept of social class needs to be rethought in much of the criminological literature if we are to begin to understand its role in the process and nature of crime.

Gangs

Youth gangs in Canada are not understood very well, due, once again to difficulties with gathering data on such groups and problems of definition. Earlier, we highlighted the importance of making distinctions between real gangs and groups of youth who are merely "hanging out" together. While police in Canada distinguish gangs by their participation in criminal activities and high level of organization, the lack of both standardized definitions and systematic strategies of gathering information make it very difficult to know how much "gang-related" crime actually occurs (Solicitor General, 1994). Moreover, scholarly research on youth gangs in Canada has been hampered by lack of good historical and contemporary statistical data on their nature and makeup. As well, there are problems with gaining access to such groups, gaining trust, and the willingness of gang members to voluntarily disclose criminal activities to researchers. Much of what the public "knows" of the nature of gang activity, then, comes from largely anecdotal accounts presented in newspapers, magazines, and the like. Other than this type of information, we really only know that they mainly exist in large urban centers, that they exist in most social, ethnic and economic categories, and that there are very few *highly organized* youth gangs in Canada (Solicitor General, 1994). In addition, although there are no systematic scholarly studies of youth gangs in Canada, particularly those examining the role of female gang members, some individuals and media maintain that youth gangs are becoming more violent, younger, increasingly include girls, involve more weapons, and are creating tremendous fear among students through violence, extortion, and drug dealing in schools (see for example Mathews 1994). A recent police survey conducted in 2002 found that 23.7% of jurisdictions in Canada reported youth gang activity in 2001, and that the estimated number of youth gangs in that year was 434. The survey also reported that the vast majority (94%) of gang members were male, almost half were under age 18, and that in terms of ethnic makeup, the largest proportion of gang members were African–Canadian, followed by First Nations and Caucasian (National Crime Prevention Centre 2007). Predictably, the report also states that those most at risk of joining gangs tend to belong to groups suffering the highest levels of inequality and social disadvantage.

Victims of Youth Crime

No discussion of young offenders would be complete without considering the victims of youth crime. Recent trends in public opinion indicate that many are dissatisfied with the apparent lack of attention paid to the role and experiences of the victim in criminal offences (Latimer and Desjardins 2008). Indeed, much of the public's dissatisfaction with the Young Offenders Act had been fueled by the perceptions that the legislation demonstrated little concern for victims who were not receiving "justice" in the form of "harsher punishments," or whose experiences as victims were not being uniformly taken into account in sentencing, although in 1995, the Act was amended to uniformly permit courts to receive victim impact statements. In this section, we will briefly consider some data on the types of people who are victimized by youth crime, their relationship to the offender, and where these acts tend to take place.

The majority of victims of violent youth crime are youth themselves and in most cases the victims knew the perpetrator as acquaintances, family members or friends. The smallest fraction of perpetrators is strangers (Ogrodnik 2008).

Table 3.6 provides a breakdown of violent offence victimizations by sex. Once again, we can see that like adult crime, youth crime is gendered, in that males are more likely to be the victims of major assaults and robbery, while females are more likely to be sexually assaulted. Moreover, the risk of violent victimization of young people increases as they get older, with youth aged 15–17 reporting the highest rates of violence of any age group. It should be noted that since these data are from police reports, and are also gathered from a subset of police services in Canada, they are underestimates of actual rates.

Unfortunately, there are no data on the victims of non-violent crimes committed by young persons, however, we can be reasonably confident that the victims of a

Table 3.6 Victims of violence by age group, sex of victim and offence type, reported to subset of police services, 2008

Sex[a]	Age group											
	<3		3–5		6–8		9–11		12–14		15–17	
	F	M	F	M	F	M	F	M	F	M	F	M
Offence												
Physical assault (*total*)	435	575	1195	480	764	1442	1459	3177	4884	7491	9317	11187
Sexual assault (*total*)	186	66	1459	978	1205	506	1546	520	3706	535	3520	392
Homicide/attempts	9	11	4	5	3	5	2	5	7	12	11	42
Robbery	12	8	6	2	8	25	38	190	326	1854	826	3550
Extortion	0	0	0	3	0	3	0	5	17	20	34	54
Criminal harassment	6	6	4	7	17	20	65	61	351	169	923	233
Uttering threats	118	123	80	89	135	161	349	501	1425	1449	2218	2064
Kidnapping/ forcible confinement	11	13	10	8	13	17	29	28	104	46	322	113
Abduction (non-parental)	20	14	10	13	23	14	45	19	51	18	11	3

Adapted from (Ogrodnik 2008, pp. 25–26)
[a] M = Male, F = Female

good portion of property crimes are store owners (in the case of theft under $5,000), and those whose homes are broken into (break and enter offences).

In this chapter we have examined some important aspects of what we know about the quality and quantity of youth crime. One of the key points made was that there are severe limitations associated with official sources of data for certain types of crimes, thus reducing our confidence in fully understanding the nature and level of youth crime in Canada. We also examined some of the advantages and disadvantages of particular methods of collecting data on crime, and the importance of understanding how to interpret statistics. One conclusion we can draw from this discussion is that good data on youth crime will require a synthesis (data triangulation) of various quantitative (e.g., the Uniform Crime Reports, victimization, and self-report surveys) and qualitative methods (e.g., ethnographies, interviews, and participant observation).

In terms of the data presented in this chapter, we have seen that contrary to most media accounts, youth are *not* getting more violent and that a significant contributor to the perception of increased youth violence lies in the category of common assault which is sensitive to changes in official responses to youths behavior.

We also examined the relevance of categories such as "race," class, and gender, and explored what we know of the ways in which these factors intersect and interact with one another. The data on male and female experiences with crime either as victims or as perpetrators also point to the reality that boys and girls, like men and women, experience the world differently, a fact that should be taken into account in theorizing and policy making in relation to youth crime.

We also briefly looked at what we know about the nature and frequency of hate-, drug-, and gang-related crimes and concluded that our knowledge about these behaviors in Canada is meagre at best.

In the next and final chapter, I want to turn briefly to the policy implications emanating from the themes discussed in this and preceding chapters.

References

Bala N (1997) Young offenders law. Irwin Law, Concord

Bala N, Carrington PJ, Roberts JV (2009) Evaluating the youth criminal justice act after five years: a qualified success. Can J Criminol Crim Justice (La Revue canadienne de criminologie et de justice pénale) 51(2):131–167

Baron SW, Hartnagel TF (2002) Street youth and labor market strain. J Crim Justice 30(6):519–533

Beattie S, Cotter A (2010) Homicide in Canada, 2009. Juristat 3(3). Statistics Canada

Bélanger A, Caron-Malenfant E, Division SCD (2005) Population projections of visible minority groups, Canada, provinces and region, 2001-2017. Statistics Canada, Demography Division

Berg B (1995) Qualitative research methods for the social sciences. Allyn & Bacon, Boston

Calverley D, Cotter A, Halla E (2010) Youth custody and community services in Canada, 2008/2009. Juristat, 30(1)

Canada (1996) Growing up in Canada: national longitudinal survey of youth. Minister of Industry, Ottawa

Canadian Centre for Justice Statistics (1998) A profile of youth justice in Canada. Statistics Canada, Ottawa

Canadian Coalition for the Rights of Children (2011) Children in the parliamentary agenda: response to budget, March 2011. Canadian Coalition for the Rights of Children

Carrington P, Moyer S (1994) Trends in youth crime and police response, pre- and post-yoa. Can J Criminol 36(1):1–28

Carrington PJ, Schulenberg JL (2005) The impact of the youth criminal justice act on police charging practices with young persons: a preliminary statistical assessment. Department of Justice Canada, Ottawa

Chesney-Lind M, Pasko L (2004) The female offender: girls, women, and crime. Sage, Thousand Oaks

Chesney-Lind M, Sheldon M (1992) Girls, delinquency and juvenile justice. Brooks/Cole, Belmont

Chui T, Tran K, Maheux H (2007) Immigration in Canada: a portrait of the foreign-born population, 2006 Census. Statistics Canada, Ottawa

Crutchfield RD, Pitchford SR (1997) Work and crime: the effects of labor stratification. Social Forces 76(1):93–118

Currie E (1993) Reckoning: drugs, the cities and the American future. Hill and Wang, New York

Daly M, Wilson M (1988) Homicide. Aldine, New York

Dauvergne M, Turner J (2010) Police-reported crime statistics in Canada, 2009. Juristat 3(2). Statistics Canada

Doob AN, Cesaroni C (2004) Responding to youth crime in Canada. University of Toronto Press, Toronto

Doob AN, Marinos V, Varma KN (1998) Youth crime and the youth justice system in Canada. University of Toronto Centre of Criminology, Toronto

Elliot D, Ageton S (1980) Reconciling race and class differences in self-reported and official estimates of delinquency. Am Sociol Rev 45:95–110

Esbensen F, Winfree LT (1998) Race and gender differences between gang and non-gang youths: Results from a multisite survey. Justice Quart 15(3):505–525

Farnworth M, Thornberry TP, Krohn MD, Lizotte AJ (1994) Measurement in the study of class and delinquency: Integrating theory with research. J Res Crime Delinq 31(1):32–61

Gabor T (1994) The suppression of crime statistics on race and ethnicity: the price of political correctness. Can J Criminol 36(2):153–163

Gaetz S (2004) Safe streets for whom? Homeless youth, social exclusion, and criminal victimization. Can J Criminol Crim Justice (La Revue Canadienne de Criminologie et de Justice Pénale) 46(4):423–456

Haapasalo J, Tremblay RE (1994) Physically aggressive boys from ages 6 to 12: family background, parenting behavior, and prediction of delinquency. J Consult Clin Psychol 62(5):1044

Hagan F (1997) Research methods in criminal justice and criminology. Allyn & Bacon, Boston

Hagan J, McCarthy B (1997) Mean streets: youth crime and homelessness. Cambridge University Press, Cambridge

Jensen E, Gerber J, Mosher C (2004) Social consequences of the war on drugs: the legacy of failed policy. Crim Justice Policy Rev 15(1):100–121

John Howard Society of Canada (2000) Submission to the Justice and Human Rights Committee of the House of Commons: Bill C-3 Youth Criminal Justice Act. John Howard Society of Canada

Juristat (1997) Canadian crime statistics. Canadian Centre for Justice Statistics, cat. No. 85-002-xpe vol 18, no. 11

La Prairie C, Griffiths CT (1984) Native juvenile delinquency: a review of recent findings. Can Legal Aid Bull 5(1):39–46

Lagier PM (1982) Juvenile delinquency to real criminality—the serious habitual delinquent. Can J Criminol 24(2):141–153

Laidler KJ, Hunt G (2001) Accomplishing femininity among the girls in the gang. Brit J Criminol 41(4):656–678

Latimer J, Desjardins N (2008) The 2008 national justice survey: tackling crime and public confidence. Department of Justice, Canada

Leblanc M (1983) Delinquency as an epiphenomenon of adolescence. In: Corrado R (ed) Current issues in juvenile justice. Buttworths, Toronto

Lowman J (1986) Street prostitution in vancouver: notes on the genesis of a social problem canadian journal of criminology. Can J Criminol 28(1):1–16

Mahony T (2011) Women and the criminal justice system: a gender-based statistical report. Statistics Canada

Mathews F (1994) Youth gangs on youth gangs. Solicitor General Canada, Ottawa

McCarthy JD, Hoge DR (1984) The dynamics of self-esteem and delinquency. Am J Sociology 90(2):396–410

Milligan S (2010) Youth court statistics, 2008/2009. Juristat. Available at http://www.statcan.gc.ca/pub/85-002-x/2010002/article/11294-eng.htm

Morin B (1990) Native youth and the young offenders act. Leg Perspect 14(4):13–15

Mosher C (1996) Minorities and misdemeanours: the treatment of black public order offenders in ontario's criminal justice system-1892–1930. Can J Criminol 38(4):413–438

National Crime Prevention Centre (2007) Youth gangs in Canada: what do we know? Public Safety Canada

Ogrodnik L (2008) Child and youth victims of police-reported violent crime, 2008. 85F0033M, No. 23. Canadian Centre for Justice Statistics

Ontario (1995) Report of the commission on systemic racism in the Ontario criminal justice system. Queens Printer, Toronto

Pate K (2008) Why do we think young women are committing more violent offences? http://www.elizabethfry.ca/violent/page1.htm

Reitsma-Street M (1993) Canadian youth court charges and dispositions for females before and after implementation of the young offenders act. Can J Criminol 35(4):437–458

Rex J (1983) Race relations in sociological theory. Routledge and Keegan Paul, London

Roberts J (2002) Racism and the collection of statistics relating to race and ethnicity. In: Chan W, Mirchandani K (eds) Crimes of colour: racialization and the criminal justice system in Canada. Broadview Press, Peterborough, pp 101–112

Savoie J (2007) Youth self-reported delinquency, Toronto 2006. Canadian Centre for Justice Statistics

Schissel B (1997) Blaming children: youth crime, moral panics and the politics of hate. Fernwood Publishing, Halifax

Statistics Canada (2001) Visible minorities in Canada. Canadian Centre for Justice Statistics Profile Series, 85F0033MIE. Statistics Canada

Statistics Canada (2005) Population projection of visible minority groups, Canada, provinces and regions: 2001–2017 (91–541-XIE). Statistics Canada, Ottawa

Tanner J (1996) Teenage troubles: youth and deviance in Canada. Nelson, Scarborough

Tanner J (2010) Teenage troubles: youth and deviance in Canada. Oxford University Press, Don Mills

Taylor-Butts A, Bressan A (2008) Youth crime in Canada, 2006. Canadian Centre for Justice Statistics

Thomas J (2008) Youth court statistics, 2006/2007. Canadian Centre for Justice Statistics

Venkatesh SA (1997) The social organization of street gang activity in an urban ghetto. Am J Sociol 103(1):82–112

West WG (1984) Young offenders and the state: a Canadian perspective on delinquency. Butterworths, Toronto

White R, Cunneen C (2006) Social Class, youth crime and justice. In: Goldson B, Muncie J (eds) Youth, crime and justice: critical issues. Sage Publications Ltd, pp 17–29

Wilson JQ, Herrnstein R (1985) Crime and human nature: the definitive study of the causes of crime. Simon and Schuster, New York

Wortley S (1999) A northern taboo: research on race, crime, and criminal justice in Canada. Can J Criminol 41(2):261–262

Wortley S (2003) Hidden intersections: research on race, crime, and criminal justice in Canada. Can Ethnic Stud 35(3):99–117

Young J (2004) Voodoo Criminology and the Numbers Game. In: Ferrell J, Hayward K, Morrison W, Presdee M (eds) Cultural criminology, unleashed. GlassHouse Press, London

Zack N (2001) Philosophical aspects of the AAA statement on "race". Anthropol Theory 1(4):445–465

Chapter 4
From Youth Justice to Social Justice

Abstract This chapter outlines some of the policy options that might be considered if Canada is to develop a more equitable and effective youth justice system. In keeping with the arguments advanced earlier, most of these policy options focus on social institutions and relationships in addition to criminal justice system ones. As such, the chapter points to the importance of linking youth justice with social justice.

By the end of the courses in criminology or criminal justice I teach, I sense that many students are feeling pretty cynical. While decades of research have shown unequivocally that crime is a complicated social problem, warranting complex solutions; unfortunately, Canada's historical approach to the problem of youth crime has been simplistic and ineffective, and it is in danger of repeating past mistakes if current trends continue.

Regardless of the pessimism we might feel after reviewing the record of Canadian youth criminal justice policies, however, workable solutions to youth crime do exist. Many of the solutions proposed in this final chapter will not be easy to implement because they require long-term fundamental changes in social structure and policy, and call for fundamental shifts in the way we think about youth and crime. Others are immediate, desirable, and certainly attainable, but they will also require political will.

In what follows, we will briefly revisit some important arguments pertaining to the failures of youth justice policies in Canada. We will then examine the extent to which current policies and practices can be retained or modified, or discarded altogether to achieve a more equitable and effective youth justice system. Finally, we will review some potential solutions to the dilemmas and issues faced by young people and the criminal justice system they face today.

S. Alvi, *Youth Criminal Justice Policy in Canada*, SpringerBriefs in Criminology,
DOI: 10.1007/978-1-4419-0273-3_4, © The Author(s) 2012

If It Doesn't Work, Do It Again

A central theme of this book is that criminal justice policies for young Canadians have generally failed to reflect the fact that crime is a process that occurs in a social context. Crime is not just an "event" perpetrated by individuals against victims. Rather, all crime has a "dynamic history." As MacLean (1996, p. 3) argues:

> crime is not a an event or a "social fact," but a social process which includes a number of social events each of which is inextricably bound up with the other. If we conceptualize crime as being an event, the violation of law by an individual, then we run the risk of focusing on that individual at the expense of comprehending the entire process. We wonder what kind of person would violate the law and conclude that something is wrong with him or her.

Thus, one of the central obstacles to achieve effective youth justice policies in Canada stems from the tendency to individualize what are, in fact, *social* problems.

Combating the tendency to view crime as an individual act divorced from the social environment continues to be one of the central challenges faced by progressive criminologists. Yet as we have seen, views on crime held by the general public, fueled by media accounts, tend to place responsibility for crime squarely on the shoulders of perpetrators. Moreover, many Canadians believe that levels of both adult and youth crime are increasing, despite evidence to the contrary deriving from both victimization surveys and official data sources.

Why do we continue to adhere to myths about crime and criminal justice? The first thing to consider in answering this question is the role of the media. As I argued earlier, media accounts exaggerate the reality of crime and are central to the creation and reproduction of "moral panics" about crime (Goode and Ben-Yehuda 1994; Muncie 1984; Schissel 1997). Also problematic is that the media often do not know anything about crime, criminal justice or, crime policy, and tend to be uncritical of political decisions made about crime (Lavrakas 1997).

But does this mean that a sheep-like public simply believes what the media tells us to believe? Probably not. Indeed, people take an active role creating their own belief systems about a host of social problems, including crime. For instance, Baron and Hartnagel (1996) have shown that a good portion of the public justify their "confidence" in, and demand for a punishment-oriented criminal justice system because they hold conservative or neo-conservative values where youth crime is viewed as a calculated, rational choice, deserving calculated, "rational" responses such as punishment and general and specific deterrence. The trouble is, of course, that these strategies have never been convincingly shown to work (Bishop 2000; Lab 1997).

Beliefs and values also exist in a social context, and at the moment, Canada is locked into a neo-conservative stance regarding economic, political, and social issues. It is not surprising, therefore, that both the Youth Criminal Justice Act and proposed amendments to it seem to favor punishment and "getting tough," in combination with "rehabilitation" strategies which pathologize the individual instead of the social system. Even more disturbing, in addition to cutting taxes which could be used to fund badly needed or decaying social programs, neo-conservative governments in Canada have been elected and re-elected partially on their skill at fanning public fear of a youth crime epidemic which does not exist, and trumpeting "get tough" solutions which do not work.

Predictably, when solutions requiring transformation of the social structure and current power relations are proposed, neo-conservatives are quick to argue that "liberal," "bleeding heart" solutions can only make the problem worse, that the costs of a structural attack on crime outweigh those of building prisons, and that criminals should be dealt with via criminal justice policy, and not social policy (Walker 1998). Yet they make these assertions without any good data of their own, and in spite of evidence that incarceration, punishment, and "getting tough" have been abject failures.

Some might ask, if so many people seem to support neo-conservative policies on crime, surely they must be right? From a scientific point-of-view, choosing to pursue policies when the evidence supporting them is weak or non-existent is pure folly. Moreover, from a moral point-of-view, conservatives are only right if it is true that social life consists *only* of freely chosen personal decisions and the responsibilities that go with them, and that ultimately, we have no obligations to others.

A related problem is that people generally look for simple solutions to complex problems, particularly if competing solutions tend to shake their world view. No wonder, then, that the public is so fascinated by the campaign to find "cures for crime" in well-established but narrowly focused professions such as medicine or psychology. As we have seen, when those seeking to understand crime assume that the answers lie *within* the individual (e.g., in "crime genes," or "dysfunctional personalities,") they presume that "treating" the individual, will suffice to eliminate or reduce crime. In effect, this shifts our attention away from social issues toward individual ones.

There are bureaucratic issues at work here too. Criminal justice typically means processing individuals through a system which is highly structured, inflexible, and divorced from other institutions, a problem Currie (1985, p. 18) has identified as "compartmentalizing social problems along bureaucratic lines."

One of the paradoxes of Canadian youth criminal justice is that the Youth Criminal Justice Act does contain strategies that could, if implemented consistently and appropriately, reduce the *impact* of crime on victims and offenders, their families, and society. What this, or any other law will *not* do, is significantly reduce the *incidence* of crime because law cannot address the original, pre-arrest, causes of criminal behavior. In short, because the law is limited in its ability to solve youth crime, we should be looking *outside* the law for solutions (Bala 1997).

The position taken in this chapter is that neo-conservatives are wrong, not only because their assumptions about the nature of society are flawed, but also because they assume that crime is a property of individuals and not social conditions and policies. Throughout this book, I have argued with Marx that while people do make their own decisions, they do not make them under conditions they have necessarily chosen themselves. Many people's lives are *structured* by social processes and forces over which they have limited or no control. Accordingly, progressive solutions to crime and other social problems hinge on our ability to understand the interplay of individual lives and social conditions. What this suggests, then, is that a truly effective youth justice system requires rethinking criminal justice in terms of *social* justice, and then acting accordingly. Does this mean that current laws and the system in which they are embedded are completely useless? The answer is no. There are some redeeming aspects of the current legislation, while other components require serious reconsideration, particularly in light of the proposed changes contained in Bill C-4.

The Potential of Extrajudicial Measures

The first component we will consider here is Extrajudicial Measures. This important piece of the justice for youth legislation contains within it the seeds of a truly progressive, and potentially very effective response to youth in conflict with the law because the philosophy of removing youth from contact with the formal system as early as possible is essentially sound (except for those who believe in a strict punishment model). However, problems such as potential net-widening, inconsistency in application across and within jurisdictions, lack of community resources, and inadequate evaluation of programs still remain. Thus, to heighten the efficacy of extrajudicial measures, we require better data on how often they are being used, more program ideas, theoretically and methodologically sound program evaluations, and less vague guidelines.

Youth Justice Committees

Although Youth Justice Committees are included as a component of the YCJA, they have received relatively little attention in the media and elsewhere as potentially more progressive ways of dealing with youth crime. These committees began in First Nation's communities as an attempt to deal with high recidivism rates among aboriginal youth offenders. They are made up of volunteers working in concert with other components of the formal criminal justice system and community-based agencies to meet the needs of young offenders within their communities, and are often responsible for the administration of alternative responses to youth transgression (Paiment 1996).

There is substantial variation (across and within provinces) in the activities of these committees, but generally, they hold the potential of restoring a sense of community responsibility for youth justice, reducing the destructive outcomes of the formal justice process, and providing communities with flexible ways of dealing with youth, thereby meeting the needs of the community.

There are, of course, dangers in using community members as the mechanism to deal with youth crime (Paiment 1996), including:

- Community members who bring an attitude of punishment and vigilantism to their work.
- The lack of resources to fund programs, and the out-of-pocket expenses incurred by committee members.
- The lack of community-based programs for youth, and limited services and programs in remote areas.
- The lack of sound evaluations of this approach.

Sentencing Circles and Reintegrative Shaming

The basic ideas behind sentencing circles are healing, peacemaking, and reintegration of the offender into mainstream society (Braithwaite 1989; Sharpe 1998). This important alternative to formal processing and sentencing is actually very old, having its roots in the practices of many Aboriginal communities (Braithwaite and Daly 1994).

As such, this perspective complements a "peacemaking" criminology framework (Caulfield 2000; Fuller 1998; Pepinsky and Quinney 1991), which asks us to consider: "....as fully as possible, the human potential for goodness, and....calls for us to recognize the commonalities and connections between ourselves and others" (Friedrichs 1991, p. 105). In effect, this approach to dealing with crime requires us to act upon the idea that individuals *as well as communities* are responsible for crime (Sharpe 1998) and that crime can only be dealt with by reconnecting community members with one another.

According to Braithwaite (1989), one of the central reasons for crime is the failure of communities to effectively "shame" their members into complying with norms. It is "social disapproval" which prevents individuals from committing crime, but communities in which individuals have lost their sense of interdependence and connection with one another are less able to exercise such forms of social control. The point is not to shame individuals, but to shame them *and* "reintegrate" them into the community.

To what extent have these principles been put into action in the Canadian context and with respect to youth? Today, there are programs in place that base themselves on some variation of the philosophy discussed above. For instance, *sentencing circles* involve community members participating in decision-making about offender sentences in conjunction with victims (Panko 2005). Other approaches within this philosophy include *healing circles*, which attempt to resolve criminal behavior before it occurs by bringing community members together, and *community circles*, which attempt to involve community members at all stages of the formal criminal justice process (Sharpe 1998).

Changes in the mandates and operations of alternative measures programs and youth justice communities, and the implementation of strategies based on reintegrating offenders could potentially go a long way to reduce the harmful effects of formal processing. Ultimately, however, such programs are post hoc. In other words, they do not allow us to address the *causes* of youth crime. A central argument of this book is that we cannot deal with youth crime appropriately if we are *only* to deal with after it has happened, no matter how progressively we do so. Accordingly, it is to an examination of preventative approaches that we turn next.

From Youth Justice to Social Justice

There will always be a role for the criminal justice system in dealing with crime. But it is no secret that preventing youth crime in society demands social-structural change, and according to at least one report, recent trends in the status of Canada's children indicate we have a long way to go (Canadian Council on Social Development 2006). Many pages could be written about social-structural change and its relationship to crime, and we do not have space here to cover all possibilities. Accordingly, in what follows, we will examine only a few dimensions of change necessary for revitalizing and rebuilding appropriate, effective responses to youth crime.

Tailoring Policies to Reflect Realities

First and foremost, we must understand that if crime is committed disproportionately by poor, disenfranchised young men, then we need to closely examine the social conditions in which they live if we are to create useful alternatives to the current system. Similarly, we need to examine the social conditions and circumstances in which young girls in conflict with the law find themselves, and take into account that there are clearly "racial" differences in the administration of youth criminal justice policies. Certainly, we must tailor our policies to reflect the needs of individuals and communities. But to do this the public must become aware of the realities of crime, and they must be given the opportunity to participate meaningfully in political decisions about crime.

One way to raise awareness is to engage in a strategy to overcome biases and inaccuracies about youth crime which are shaped and regurgitated by the media. To do this, criminologists must become more credible spokespeople about crime (Barak 1988), and engage in "newsmaking criminology," a strategy which involves "actively challenging silences, identifying omissions, and resurrecting the eliminated through participating in the making of news stories" (Henry and Milovanovic 1996, p. 216).

If people are better informed about crime, they will be more likely to demand policies that reflect realities. At the same time, politicians are less likely to prey upon public fears of youth (or adult) crime if they know that an informed electorate is reluctant to listen to misleading claims about the causes of crime and what is to be done about it.

Better Support for Families and Children

We have seen in several places in this book that youth crime is very much an outcome of the intersection of social structural and familial factors. We know, for instance, that poverty, unemployment, welfare dependency, lack of opportunities, and community resources as well as racism create "criminogenic" conditions. As well, mental, physical and sexual abuse, inadequate supervision, excessively harsh, lax, or inconsistent discipline and family violence, and poor school performance, among other factors, all contribute to youth crime. What is to be done about these issues?

This is a difficult question to answer because it entails examining the complex ways in which such factors work together to create the conditions under which some youth may commit crime. For example, while it is true that inadequate parental attention is correlated with delinquency, this does not mean, as neo-conservatives suggest, that the solution to youth crime is to focus only on training "better parents" and certainly, it does not require that parents should be punished for the actions of their children. Parenting in modern Canadian society, like many other post-industrial societies, involves managing competing demands, high levels of stress, decreasing time for meaningful family interaction, and declining resources for families in general. Hence, if we are to expect to improve the quality of parenting in our society, we will need to address the social conditions that modern families find themselves in (Schaffner 1997).

Two of the most important things we can do to create a better experience for children now, and in the future, is to implement a nationally funded child care system in Canada, and to encourage employers to help their employees negotiate competing work and family obligations. The benefits of this two-pronged approach are;

- Many women cannot work at all, or are restricted to low-paying, dead-end jobs because they do not have access to affordable, high quality child care. A nationally funded child care system would increase the chances that these women, many of whom are single parents, could enter the paid labor force and thereby improve the economic conditions of their families.
- A nationally funded, universal child care program would be more able to deliver high quality services to a larger proportion of the Canadian population than existing child care models. As the Ontario Ministry of Community and Social Services, (Ontario 1990, p. 20) points out, "quality child care programs [can act]

as a preventative measure against poor school performance and emotional and behaviorial problems, particularly for poor children, regardless of whether their parents are working."

Although adequate child care is important, it is only part of the problem families are facing. Increasingly, scholars are urging us to look at the larger economic context in which children and families exist. And when we do so, it is clear that changing work conditions, the "disappearance" and reconfiguration of work, declines in real wages, and disappearing or diminishing social programs are all contributing to major stresses faced by contemporary families. When we look at why these conditions have come to pass, it is clear that they are outcomes of a society which values its members only insofar as they can compete (on the "global stage" if you like current cliches), as individuals, and without complaining when they "fail to make the grade."

In a nutshell, the new realities of parent-family interaction are for many youth the outcomes of larger global economic processes about which they can do nothing. On the other hand, it is certainly within the power of adults, particularly powerful ones, to take responsibility for managing the impact of rapid economic change on children and families. But doing so will require adults to truly recognize that the emotional, physical, and psychological care of children should take precedence over enhanced corporate profits.

What about schooling? As one of the primary socialization agents, schools play a very important role in preparing children for life in the adult world. Moreover, lack of meaningful school experiences affect a child's life-chances, and increase their participation in risk taking behaviors. Clearly, changes in the nature of schooling and education must be made. In particular, we need to make the schools more responsive to the needs of contemporary children, but this is unlikely to happen in today's environment where teachers are demoralized, pupil–teacher ratios are high, funding is being cut for "special needs," and curricula are revised to reflect the cult of competitive individualism.

Rethinking Criminal Justice Spending

Spending public money on social problems such as crime should reflect both our understanding of the problem, and the priorities we value in solving them. In 2008 Canada spent nearly 1 billion dollars on youth corrections alone, nearly 9 billion dollars on police, and nearly more than half a billion dollar each on courts and prosection (Zhang 2008), which begs the question, how much money *should* we be spending on youth justice, and what should it be spent on? This is a question that can only be answered after an honest evaluation of our priorities. Consider, for example, that although incarceration is, to say the least, an inadequate response to youth crime, it is extraordinary that we would continue to spend money on incarceration when that money could be diverted to community development and assisting families and children experiencing difficulty managing everyday life.

Table 4.1 Selected government transfer payments to persons in millions of dollars, 2004–2008

	Year				
	2004	2005	2006	2007	2008
	Millions of dollars				
Federal					
Family and youth allowances	157	165	187	205	210
Unemployment insurance benefits	13,269	12,937	12,498	12,561	13,325
Scholarships and research grants	734	789	858	883	922
Provincial					
Social assistance, income maintenance	6,788	6,918	7,123	7,480	7,821
Social assistance, other	3,167	3,445	3,791	3,989	4,201
Workers compensation benefits	5,083	5,229	5,316	5,500	5,749
Grants to benevolent associations	9,011	9,581	10,593	11,280	11,745

Source Adapted from Statistics Canada, CANSIM table at http://www40.statcan.gc.ca/l01/cst01/govt05a-eng.htm

Compare, for instance, levels of spending on justice components such as policing and corrections, compared with federal spending on transfer payments such as social assistance and family and youth allowances (Table 4.1). Clearly, Canadian governments seem content to spend nearly as much (and in some categories of spending such as family and youth allowances or scholarships) on post hoc "solutions" to crime as they are on programs that could prevent the occurrence of criminal behavior in the first place.

Reducing Poverty and Inequality

Perhaps the most challenging strategy considered here is the reduction of poverty and all forms of inequality. Reducing poverty is the most important crime-fighting strategy there is because it directly or indirectly shapes criminogenic factors such as access to education, the quality of education, diminished parental authority, and communities which lack cohesion (Reiman 1998). Among the approaches that could be pursued in this regard are;

- Job creation and training programs that meet the needs of individuals and fit with the new reality that the nature and type of work available in our society has changed dramatically. More specifically, we should be focusing on the possibilities offered by the creation of a "social economy"—one that allows people to contribute to their communities by emphasizing paid and volunteer community service for which governments pay a "shadow" wage (For a detailed discussion, see Rifkin 1996). Moreover, greater attention has to be paid to important issues such as:
- Higher minimum wage levels and a guaranteed minimum income.
- More housing assistance.

- Nationally funded, universal child care.
- Giving youth a better stake in the adult world by introducing entrepreneurial skills into the high school curriculum, and making the school to work transition a more realistic and meaningful experience.
- Creating better linkages between schools, private business, and government agencies.

These and similar initiatives would help to improve social conditions while reducing gender, class, and ethnic inequality in our society. One other related area where great improvements could be made is community cohesion. Many youth crimes are related to boredom, lack of opportunities, poor role models, and lack of social cohesion in local communities. Recent research by Robert J. Sampson and his colleagues (Morenoff et al. 2001; Sampson 2003, 2006), has shown that neighborhoods with high levels of *collective efficacy* tend to have lower rates of crime than those with lower levels. Here, collective efficacy is defined as "mutual trust among neighbors combined with a willingness to intervene on behalf of the common good, specifically to supervise children and maintain public order" (Sampson et al. 1998, p. 1). What this suggests, then, is that in communities where people are willing to converse with, support, help, and otherwise "look out for" their neighbors and their children, youth crime could be greatly reduced.

Finally, we must avoid the drift toward the "adultification" of youth crime, a situation in which the treatment of youth more and more closely resembles the treatment accorded to adults (Goldson 2011), and is characterized by harsh, punitive and exclusionary penalties in a context of zero tolerance (Benekos and Merlo 2008). We need to listen to youthful concerns and respond positively and coherently to those whose social and economic environments place them at disadvantage and risk.

This book has focused on solutions to youth crime from the standpoint of "critical criminology." It has emphasized that much of the youth crime problem stems from public and political misunderstanding of the realities of crime at the very least, and quite likely, from deliberate manipulation of "the facts" for political or other gain.

Only a handful of progressive policies and practices are discussed here to create a more equitable, and effective youth justice system, but in addition, key social-structural transformations must be taken seriously if we are to ever create a realistic response to crime. The main argument here and elsewhere in this book is we have not made a genuine effort to understand youth crime in terms of the lives of youth themselves. Moreover, we have failed to act upon the truth that our society is criminogenic, and continues to be so, choosing instead to blame children for adult failures (Eisler and Schissel 2008). Current approaches to law and order among youth in Canada pathologize and individualize children. Unless we honestly re-think crime, its context, and the policies and practices that *should* emerge from this knowledge, we are doomed to repeat the mistakes of the past.

References

Bala N (1997) Young offenders law. Irwin Law, Concord, Ontario

Barak G (1988) News-making criminology: reflections on the media, intellectuals, and crime. JQ 5(4):565–588

Baron S, Hartnagel T (1996) "Lock 'em up": attitudes toward punishing juvenile offenders. Canadian Journal of Criminology 38(2):191–212

Benekos PJ, Merlo AV (2008) Juvenile justice: the legacy of punitive policy. Youth Violence and Juvenile Justice 6(1):28–46

Bishop DM (2000) Juvenile offenders in the adult criminal justice system (27). University of Chicago Press, Chicago

Braithwaite J (1989) Crime shame and reintegration. Cambridge University Press, New York

Braithwaite J, Daly K (1994) Masculinities, violence and communitarian control. In: Newburn T (ed) Just boys doing business? Men masculinities and crime. Routledge, London, pp 189–213

Canadian Council on Social Development. (2006). The progress of Canada's children and youth 2006. Canadian Council on Social Development

Caulfield SL (2000) Creating peaceable schools. N 267RN Annals of the American Academy of Political and Social Science, 567, 170–185

Currie E (1985) Confronting Crime: An American challenge. Pantheon, New York

Eisler L, Schissel B (2008) Globalization, justice and the demonization of youth. Int J Soc Inq 1(1):167–187

Friedrichs DO (1991) Peacemaking criminology in world filled with conflict. In: MacLean BD (ed) New directions in critical criminology. Collective Press, Vancouver, BC, pp 101–106

Fuller JR (1998) Criminal justice: A peacemaking perspective. Allyn and Bacon, Boston

Goldson B (2011). 'Time for a fresh start', but is this it? A critical assessment of the report of the independent commission on youth crime and antisocial behavior. Youth Justice 11(1):3

Goode E, Ben-Yehuda N (1994) Moral panics: culture, politics and social construction. Annu Rev of Soc 20:149–171

Henry S, Milovanovic D (1996) Constitutive crimimology: Beyond postmodernism. Sage, London

Lab S (1997) Crime prevention: Approaches, practices and evaluationss. Anderson, Cincinatti

Lavrakas PJ (1997) Politicians, journalists, and the rhetoric of the 'crime prevention' public policy debate. In: Lab SP(ed) Crime prevention at a crossroads. Anderson Publishing Co, Cincinatti

MacLean BD (1996) Crime and society: Readings in critical criminology. Copp Clark, Toronto

Morenoff JD, Sampson RJ, Raudenbush SW (2001) Neighborhood inequality, collective efficacy, and the spatial dynamics of violence. Criminology 39(3):517–559

Muncie J (1984) The trouble with kids today. Hutchinson, Dover

Ontario, Ministry of Community and Social Services (1990) Ontario child health study: children at risk. Toronto, Ontario: Queen's printer for Ontario

Paiment, R. (1996) An exploratory study of youth justice committees. Technical report, department of justice Canada, research, statistics and evaluation directorate, policy sector, tr1996-8e.

Panko C (2005) R. V. TDP: A young offender, his sentencing circle, and the YCJA. Saskatchewan Law Review 68:455–474

Pepinsky H, Quinney R (1991) Criminology as peacemaking. Indiana University Press, Bloomingto

Reiman J (1998) The rich get richer and the poor get prison: ideology, class, and criminal justice (5), Allyn and Bacon, Boston

Rifkin J (1996) The End of Work: The decline of the global labor force and the dawn of the post-market era. Tarcher/Putnam, New York

Sampson RJ (2003) The neighborhood context of well-being. Perspect in Biol and Med, 46(3):53

Sampson RJ (2006) Collective efficacy theory: lessons learned and directions for future inquiry. Taking stock: the status of criminological theory 15:149–167

Sampson RJ, Raudenbush SW and Earls F (1998) Neighborhood collective efficacy—does it help reduce violence?. Nat Inst of Justice

Schaffner L (1997) Families on probation: court ordered parenting skills classes for parents of juvenile offenders. Crime Delinquency 43(4):412–437

Schissel B (1997) Blaming children: Youth crime, moral panics and the politics of hate. Fernwood Publishing, Halifax

Sharpe S (1998) Restorative justice: A vision for healing and change. Edmonton victim-offender mediation society, Edmonton

Walker S (1998) Sense and nonsense about crime and drugs: a policy guide. West/Wadsworth, Belmont

Zhang T (2008) Costs of crime in Canada. Department of Justice Canada